Jim,

It's the best book I found
and still not good enough.
hope it will bring you over

Amnon

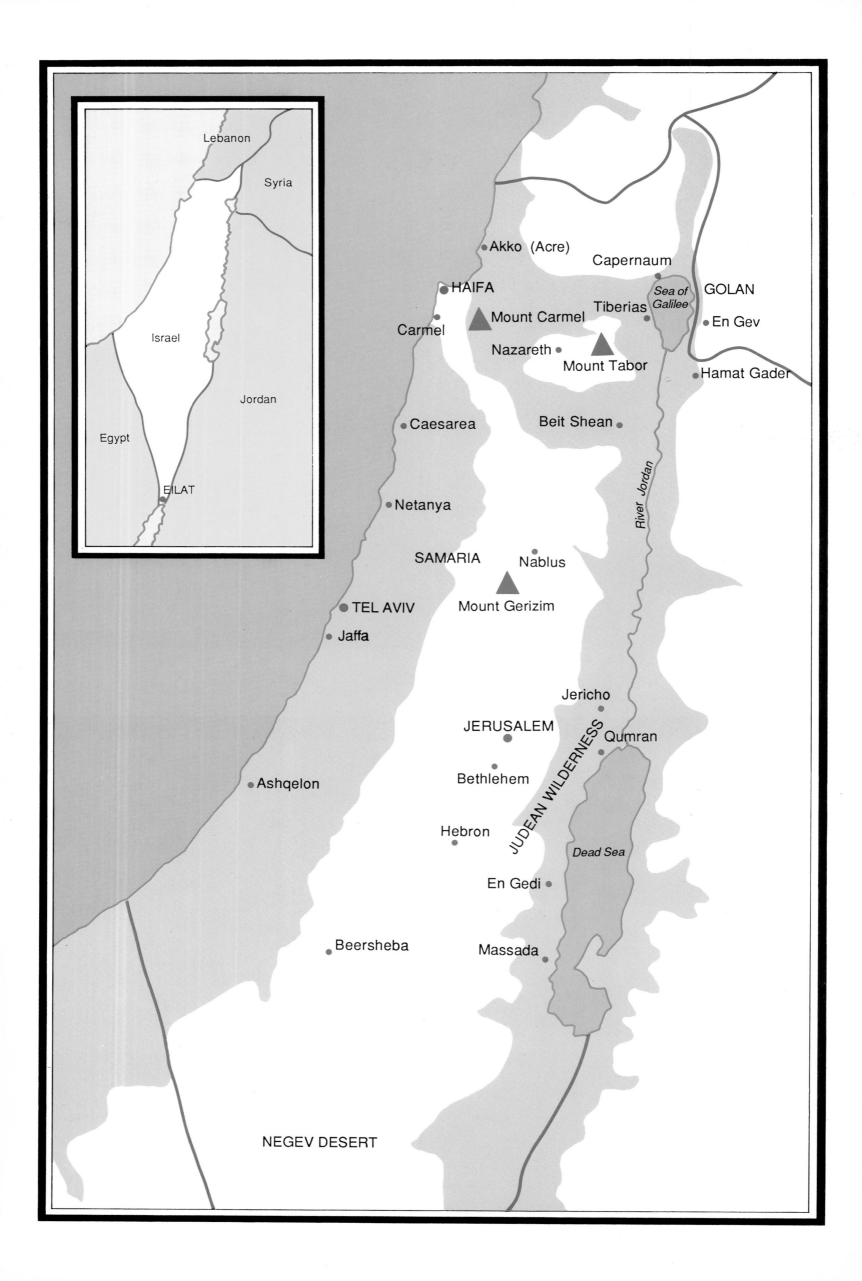

Lebanon

Syria

Israel

Jordan

Egypt

EILAT

Akko (Acre)

Capernaum

HAIFA

Sea of
Galilee

GOLAN

Mount Carmel

Tiberias

En Gev

Carmel

Nazareth

Mount Tabor

Hamat Gader

Caesarea

Beit Shean

River Jordan

Netanya

SAMARIA

Nablus

Mount Gerizim

TEL AVIV

Jaffa

Jericho

JERUSALEM

Qumran

Bethlehem

JUDEAN WILDERNESS

Ashqelon

Hebron

Dead Sea

En Gedi

Beersheba

Massada

NEGEV DESERT

ISRAEL

Text by
ROGER BAKER

Photography by
RICHARD T. NOWITZ

CRESCENT BOOKS
NEW YORK

To my wife Varda, whose support was unending, and my children Daniella and Abe, whose love and laughter filled my heart.

CLB 2179
© 1988 Colour Library Books Ltd., Godalming, Surrey, England.
All rights reserved.
Printed and bound in Barcelona, Spain by Cronion, S.A.
Colour separations by Hong Kong Graphic Arts Ltd, Hong Kong.
Published in 1988 by Crescent Books, distributed by Crown Publishers, Inc.
ISBN 0 517 66294 9
h g f e d c b a

Arrival

When the plane touches down at Ben Gurion Airport some of the passengers break into spontaneous applause. When they disembark into that humid, hothouse heat some kneel down and kiss the earth.

It is a mixed collection of travellers; tourists making for the sun-drenched beaches and magical underwater world of Eilat; archaeologists bound for one of the many digs in this most historic of countries; young people eager for their first taste of life on a kibbutz; slightly nervous middle-aged couples visiting relatives they may not have seen for a decade or more; whole families, from grandmothers to babes-in-arms, about to start a completely new life in what they have always known to be their homeland.

By the time passport control, security checks and all the other formalities are finished it is growing dark, and by the time we are speeding towards Jerusalem it is night. The car's headlights show a motorway which, apart from the roadsigns in Hebrew and Arabic, could be anywhere in Europe – France, Germany, the United

Top pictures: a Bedouin in Eilat (remaining pictures), Israel's southernmost port. Overlooked by the rugged mountains of Jordan, Saudi Arabia and the Sinai, with its shores washed by the warm blue waters of the Red Sea, Eilat is also one of the country's most exciting and popular holiday resorts.

Kingdom. Like all Israelis, our driver is exuberantly welcoming, eager to start showing off the wonders of his country at once.

'That's Samson's village over there ...' he gestures into the darkness. And, later, 'Abraham was born down in that valley ...' and when we reach Jerusalem (higher, cooler) he insists we first admire the great modern buildings, the Hebrew University and the Knesset, Israel's parliament outside which a flame burns constantly in honour of the country's soldiers dead in various wars.

Thus, within an hour or so of arrival, the visitor is bombarded with the complexities and contrasts of a country which has many layers, which is as ancient as the rocks of Masada and as modern as the jets which fly overhead. The crowded, bustling markets and multi-

textured deserts remind us we are on the threshold of the mysterious, glamorous Orient; the modern hotels and glittering department stores indicate the familiar characteristics of western cities.

As he explores the country, the traveller will be constantly struck by these contrasts – in the land itself, in the cities, in the people. There are stretches of bleak, seemingly endless desert and richly fertile valleys boosted by the massive, high-tech irrigation schemes. There are tiny villages which are probably much the same as they were in biblical times, and modern, teeming towns.

Native-born Israelis are called Sabras – which is actually a prickly pear! But the name has wisdom as well as wit; the pear's exterior may be tough with sharp edges, but inside, the fruit is mellow and sweet. This sums up the challenge of Israel and its people.

The importance of Eilat (these pages) as a major port waned with the opening of the Suez Canal to Israeli shipping. The town saved its economy, however, by turning to tourism and making the most of its fantastic weather and natural attractions, which include the richly varied marine life of the Red Sea.

The Negev: Eilat to Beersheba

For the visitor, most of Israel's most powerful attractions tend to be concentrated in the northern part of the country, in the fertile corridor between the Mediterranean coast to the west and the Jordan Valley, which snakes down from the heights of Mount Hermon to the eerie

waters of the Dead Sea, to the east.

It is here that both the atmospheric historical and biblical sites are found as well as the busy, populous cities of the modern state. And yet a good half of the country's landmass lies to the south, making up the huge inverted triangle of desert called the Negev.

To make an exact definition of the boundaries of this region is not really possible, but for all practical purposes it is accepted that the northern border of the triangle lies just to the north of Beersheba. The border with Egypt to the west and that with Jordan to the east slowly narrow and eventually form the tip of the triangle at the Gulf of Eilat, which is an extension of the Red Sea. On this tip stands Eilat itself, Israel's most southerly town.

Separated as it is from the country's heartland by the forbidding stretches of the Negev, Eilat can be seen as a very modern kind of oasis – a virtually purpose-built holiday resort dedicated to days pursuing an exciting range of water sports or just lazing in the sun, and to evenings of good eating, drinking and dancing. There is nowhere else quite like Eilat in Israel and the town is a prime focus for visitors from all over Europe.

It is easy enough to reach Eilat, by air or overland, from Tel Aviv and Jerusalem, but visitors bent on holidaymaking tend to fly there direct, seeing nothing of the rest of the country. Many Israelis regret this since Eilat is not really typical of the country, having been created over a comparatively short space of time from an important but undistinguished port to a semi-tropical playground.

Tourist guides will always try to find a biblical mention of all towns and sites in Israel – often on somewhat tenuous evidence. Eilat, for example, is said to be Etzion Geber, which was King Solomon's gateway to Africa and where the Queen of Sheba is supposed to have landed. Accurate or not, it is certainly true that Eilat stands at an important point and, until the Suez Canal was opened up to Israeli shipping, was a significant port. Today, of course, ships can go directly to the Mediterranean ports in the north.

Below: ships of the desert under a clear blue sky and (facing page) the ruins of the ancient settlement of Qumran, on the northwestern shores of the Dead Sea. It was here, in 1947, that a Bedouin shepherd came across the first fragments of the Dead Sea Scrolls, the world's oldest known biblical manuscripts.

The ruins of Qumran (above), once the home of the ancient Essene sect, contain the scriptorium where the Dead Sea Scrolls where written. Fragments of these scrolls, comprising all but one of the books of the Old Testament, were found in the Qumran caves (top right and facing page). Top left and right: the Timna Valley, north of Eilat, the site of King Solomon's 3,000-year-old copper mines.

It was this loss of port status that made pure tourism so important to the town and its economy. Ironically, it is also Eilat's strategic position which has helped to establish it as a fascinating resort. Poised between two deserts, flanked by the mountains of Jordan and Sinai and gazing southwards across the intensely blue-green waters of the Gulf it is at once glamorous and slightly raffish.

The town, with its modern hotels, tourist centres and administrative buildings is, frankly, not particularly attractive. The glamour comes from the Gulf of Eilat itself. The limpid, transparent waters offer the visitor a unique chance to study the wonders of underwater life with their range of magnificent tropical fish and exquisite coral formations. For Europeans, Eilat is the nearest

tropical resort we have, and anyone from the most timid to the most adventurous can exploit its richness to the full.

There is, for example, the Underwater Observatory, which allows one actually to walk down a stair into the sea and watch, through special observation windows, the spectacular tropical fish. At the Coral Beach Nature Reserve all the equipment needed for actual swimming and snorkel diving is available. Full-scale deep-sea diving is available, too, with expert tuition and guidance. Extremely popular are the glass-bottomed boats which allow one to glide silently and gracefully over these colourful depths. Among the various visual

delights are the different kinds of coral, ranging from the stony reef-building kind to the delicate soft corals that seem to be suspended in the water, moving gently like fragile ferns. Among the reefs lurk giant clams and sea urchins, there are spectacular parrotfish and lionfish (with their poisonous spines), the moray eel and the small, darting butterfly fish.

Further out, in the open sea, are tuna, barracuda, various kinds of shark (including the tiger shark), sea turtles and octopus. There is, too, wind-surfing, waterskiing and swimming. There are yacht excursions all the time, and those which operate in the evening offer gourmet dinners and sometimes dancing on the trip.

This is the glamour of Eilat, a magical, other-worldly feeling floating on this sub-tropical sea watching the surrounding deserts lose their daytime harshness as the sun sets and their glaring colours slowly modulate into soft, romantic shades of pink, rose, delicate blues and ochres. The Jordanian town of Aqaba twinkles across the bay and the evenings are deliciously warm.

For the historically or archaeologically minded, there are a few tours available from Eilat. There are the remains of a Crusader Fort off Coral Island (itself a popular venue for swimming and diving), and it is possible to visit Mount Sinai and St Catherine's Monastery, which contains early Christian relics. Border formalities are made quite simple for the tourist today.

Between Eilat and Beersheba lies the Negev desert. The first view of this grand but bleak and rugged region comes as a surprise to those who imagine a desert consists of gently undulating sand dunes! There is sand in the Negev, but rather more dust. Habitation is sparse and the few roads wind tortuously through a battered landscape of eroded cliffs with great heaps of shale scree and fallen boulders. It is grimly impressive and visitors unfamiliar with this kind of terrain are constantly reminded to make sure their motorcars are

Facing page bottom left: a Bedouin camp in the awesome Negev Desert (these pages). Here, wind and sand erosion and a range of mineral deposits have created strange forms and subtle colouration, while geological action has caused such phenomena as the Large Crater (facing page top). Of historical interest is the partly-restored Byzantine town of Avdat (this page), built by Nabateans in the 2nd century.

in good condition and with full tanks; also that there is an adequate supply of drinking water on board.

Closer exploration reveals pockets of fertility. Israel's magnificent irrigation schemes have penetrated the Negev; there are crops and desert plants thriving among the inhospitable hills. There are several modern Kibbutzim here, the most famous being Sde Boker. This is celebrated because the architect of modern Israel and its distinguished Prime Minister David Ben Gurion and his wife Paula lived there until his death in 1973. The basic cottage where they lived remains as it was and has become a place of pilgrimage.

The couple are buried near the Kibbutz at the Sde Boker Institute (where scientists work in such fields as solar energy and biology). The two simple stone monuments lie peacefully in an olive grove overlooking the gorge of Nahal Zin and beyond to the spectacular reddish-brown escarpments of the desert.

From the Sde Boker Institute a gravel path winds down to one of the most delightful and impressive sights of this part of the Negev – Ein Avdat. The word 'Ein' or sometimes 'En' means 'spring' and when found in a place name guarantees an oasis or pool. Ein Avdat is a chalk canyon which acts as a natural channel for the torrential floodwaters that occasionally rage through the Negev after a storm. The ground is too dry to absorb the water and pools remain there permanently. As a result, this is an oasis of rich plant and animal life and is a national park.

The canyon itself is impressive and one may walk along the dry river bed between its walls. Vast caverns and weird shapes have

Beer Sheva, where Abraham brought his sheep for water 4,000 years ago and Bedouins still bring livestock to market (above), is in fact a haven of modernity and progress in the wild Negev Desert. Top right: Ben-Gurion's grave at Sede Boqer, (above right) the library of Ben-Gurion University (right). Facing page: the sacred city of Hebron is dominated by the Mosque of Abraham (top), which was built over the Cave of Machpelah containing the Tombs of the Patriarchs (bottom) Abraham, Isaac and Jacob.

been carved by water and weather in the walls and the rocks are covered in flowers. There are two pools and a waterfall, where it is possible to watch gazelle and ibex come down the cliffs to drink.

The ancient town of Avdat lies a few miles to the south, and here again there are spectacular limestone caves and rock sculptures, and also burial recesses, since Avdat was once a notable settlement, built by the Nabateans in the 2nd century. At that time it was an

The Dead Sea (these pages), the lowest body of water on the earth, is up to ten times more saline than other seas and is lent a strange beauty by the salt sculptures rising from its blue-green waters. Many tourists are attracted by its curative properties, and by the black, healing mud found on the beach at Ein Gedi (right).

important station for the spice routes coming from Arabia to the Mediterranean ports. Most of the relics here are from the later Roman and Byzantine periods, with an acropolis and cave dwellings in the cliff face. The Nabateans found methods of harnessing flood-waters and developed extensive farming methods. In recent years these have been reconstructed, and from the top of the town can be seen the green fields and orchards created by the ancient but now restored irrigation systems. There is also an interesting Roman bath house, with steam room and hot air vents.

It has been pointed out that the Negev has changed more in the past forty years than it had done since the days of the Roman

occupation. The location of industries, the establishment of army bases and deliberate improvement of towns, plus ever more sophisticated irrigation systems, seem to be proving David Ben Gurion's belief that the Negev was the clue to Israel's future prosperity.

However, when set in proportion to the actual size of the territory, these developments make little impact on the traveller. The Negev remains a formidable, impressive and sometimes awe-inspiring tract of desert. For centuries it has been the home of the wandering Bedouin nomads, and they remain, with their camel trains and herds of voracious black goats (which actually climb trees in search of food).

The capital of the Negev is Beersheba which is, today, a modern, thriving city and the southernmost large city in the country. Traces of human habitation have been unearthed which date back some 6,000 years, so it always had importance, partly because it was on the border of the more settled agricultural lands of the north and partly because it was a major station on the route into Egypt. The town has strong biblical associations: Isaac and Jacob and, according to Genesis, Abraham, who gave the place its name.

That sense of contrast which characterises so much of Israel can be experienced here. The old town of Beersheba is worth exploring, especially the amazing Bedouin market held weekly. Abraham's Well can be visited and something of the ancient atmosphere can be sniffed. But modern Beersheba is also impressive, with its exciting buildings, new university and concert hall. The town contains some of the most imaginative and forward-looking modern architecture in the country. It is well worth taking time to join one of the conducted tours round the Ben Gurion University. To the northeast of Beersheba stands the monument to the fighters who fell in the Negev during the War of Independence.

Facing page: the Dead Sea Works, where minerals are extracted from the brine with the aid of solar power. Bounded on the west by the Judaean Desert and on the east by the Mountains of Moab (below), the 100 million-year-old Dead Sea (these pages) is one of the most scenic of Israel's tourist attractions and also one of the healthiest. The beach at Ein Gedi (below) is rich in therapeutic mud (right) which can alleviate muscular and joint problems.

Travelling

The bus for Tel Aviv would pass the Kibbutz gate at 08.15 we were told. To be on the safe side we pitched ourselves and our bags fifteen minutes earlier. The Amiad Kibbutz is just to the north of the Sea of Galilee in pleasant agricultural country. It was a fine, bright morning and in the distance the Golan Heights emerged from the mist. The bus eventually appeared at 09.00.

Provided you are not encumbered by an enormous amount of luggage, travelling by bus is one of the best ways of getting around Israel. The services are frequent, inexpensive and the buses comfortable – if sometimes very crowded. It is an ideal way to meet people and it is amazing how the various languages used (French, English, Hebrew, Arabic) seem no sort of barrier to friendly communication. The Israelis are friendly, curious people and will jump straight into the kind of personal conversation which more reserved westerners might take a day or two of acquaintance to get around to.

Our bus journey from Amiad to Tel Aviv took three hours. At each stop passengers left and others arrived, seats became free and conversations were struck up. There are always young soldiers (male and female) travelling, intensely proud of their role and eager for information about the rest of the world. Snacks are shared and full details of the places you must visit are passed on at length.

Many of the most interesting sights in the country, however, are not easily reached by public transport, so if travelling independently (that is, not on an organized tour) then car hire is a solution. Roads are variable – those in the north of the country much better than those

Tall date palms (bottom) flourish in the kibbutz at Ein Gedi (this page), where an oasis nourishes luxuriant trees and flowers. This lushness provides a welcome respite from the normally barren terrain around the Dead Sea, such as the parched Judaean Mountains (facing page bottom), one of which, the Sedom Mountain (facing page top), is formed entirely of salt.

which cross desert areas, for example. Constant vigilance is necessary – where a European might expect a hard shoulder he is likely to find soft sand. Nor are the Israelis themselves famous for being expert drivers (something they seem, rather endearingly, to be proud of) so careful driving is in order.

Trains are rarely seen in Israel, since rail links cover only a small part of the country. However, the dedicated traveller might like to know that there is a good service between Tel Aviv and Haifa which passes through the main coastal towns. Another link, between Haifa and Jerusalem, is slow but takes one through some astonishingly beautiful country with memorable scenery.

Internal air flights mainly link Eilat with Tel Aviv, Haifa and Jerusalem. It is the easiest and quickest way of getting to the resort, of course, but denies one the opportunity of seeing the country and

This page: the Ein Gedi oasis, with its silvery waterfall (facing page) plunging into David's Well. One of the ancient Judaean cities, Ein Gedi, which means the 'fountain of the kid', is mentioned often in the Bible and was famed for its fragrant flowers in Solomon's day. A poet in the Song of Songs writes 'my beloved is to me a cluster of henna blossoms in the vineyards of Ein Gedi'.

meeting a variety of people.

Several bus companies run conducted tours to major tourist attractions which can last for just an afternoon or for several days (with accommodation and meals included). They are well organised and hosted by informed (and licensed) guides.

The Dead Sea: Qumran, Ein Gedi, Masada

Remote, eerie, possibly a touch frightening. Exciting, moving, awe-inspiring. Stark, bleak, threatening. Flowers, date palms, waterfalls. Sun-bathing, swimming, floating effortlessly and reading the newspaper at the same time. The shore of the Dead Sea does not offer just one experience but many – often at the same time!

The eastern border of Israel is defined by what is technically

known as the Afro-Syrian rift. This long, dramatic gash in the face of the earth is such a significant feature of the territory it is worth a moment's thought. Almost 6,500 km long, it cuts across Turkey, Syria and Israel and follows the Gulf of Eilat into Africa right down to the Zambesi River. As far as Israel is concerned, this great valley cuts its swathe from the Golan Heights in the north, provides the bed for the River Jordan and, on the way, basins for Sea of Galilee and for the Dead Sea.

Here it is deep. In fact, the Dead Sea is the lowest point on earth, being some 400 meters below sea-level. Most travellers will probably approach the Dead Sea from Jerusalem, and the drop is astonishing. Jerusalem is about 750 meters above sea-level.

The road winds down the escarpments from the Desert of Judaea

which are a feature of the district it is easy to imagine at least one that could be Lot's wife, reportedly turned into a pillar of salt.

This industrial landscape has a weird charm of its own, mainly because it is so remote and provides the only human activity in an endless perspective of bleak desert land. There is, incidentally, a similar plant in Jordan on the opposite bank of the sea.

But the Dead Sea is far from dead in reality. It's name derives from the fact that, owing to its extremely high salt content (eight times the concentration of ordinary sea water) no animal or plant life inhabits the waters. However, these waters have achieved a high therapeutic reputation, and the local climate seems to have beneficial effects on a range of disorders from skin problems to rheumatism and bronchial diseases. One of the given reasons is that, because the Dead Sea

One of the most striking sights in the Dead Sea area is the hilltop fort of Masada (these pages), built by Herod the Great in 36 BC. Here, in AD 73, a number of Jews made a desperate last stand against the Romans and, rather than be captured, committed mass suicide. Top left: a cablecar to the fort, (above left) a bathhouse in Herod's palace and (above) one of the fort's water cisterns.

in a series of tight hairpin bends and occasionally one has the unnerving experience of seeing jets screaming up the valley below the level of your car or bus!

This drop can also mean unexpected changes in climate. During the Mediterranean winter, for example, Jerusalem may be cold and wet – but half an hour away the sun shines in semi-tropical warmth. In the sumer, temperatures around the Dead Sea can rise to over 100°F but, since humidity is quite low, this need not be particularly uncomfortable. All visitors are urged, however, to drink plenty of water and all the principle tourist sights are well-equipped with water fountains.

The Dead Sea is 55 km long and was created some 100 million years ago. It is believed, however, that the southern section, which is much shallower than the rest, is of rather more recent origin and was formed at the time of the great natural upheaval that destroyed the cities of Sodom and Gomorrah as reported in the Bible. This southern section is now mostly industrial, dominated by the Dead Sea Chemical Works, which represents one of Israel's chief industries and is engaged in extracting phosphates and other chemicals from the waters.

Today there are no traces at all of what might have been the infamous Cities of the Plain, but among the rock salt formations

is so far below sea level, harmful (UVB) ultraviolet rays from the sun cannot penetrate to it, whereas the long-range, health-giving rays (UVA) can. Sunbathing is, therefore, extremely safe and healthy.

It is also believed that the high concentration of bromides in the water, and in the atmosphere itself, is a natural sedative. As a result there are many spas, health resorts and luxury hotels catering specifically for those who are recuperating or convalescing. The town of Arad overlooking the sea from a height of 1,000 meters is popular with asthma sufferers, but the main group of hotels is clustered on the shore, where the Zohar Hot Springs, thermal suphur springs with a valuably high magnesium content, can also be found. This water is radioactive, by the way.

Commanding panoramic views of Jerusalem, the Dead Sea and the Judaean Desert, the ruined fort of Herodion (this page) was built by Herod in the 1st century. Not far away, clinging to the walls of a steep canyon, is the splendid Mar Saba Monastery (facing page), the present structure of which was built in the mid-1800s by the Russians.

From Zohar to Kallia, at the northern end of the sea, the road follows the shoreline, often slightly higher than beach level. The views are spectacular with, on one side, the sheet of shimmering dark blue water and, on the other, the red, gold and ochre cliff and escarpments etched against a brilliant sky. A casual glance suggests a bleak emptiness, but this is deceptive – it is, in fact, a rich and rewarding area with stupendous historical monuments and superbly luxurious oases.

Driving to the Dead Sea from Jerusalem the road crosses an arid plain and then turns to follow the coast road at Kallia, which is a pleasant spot to pause and perhaps take one's first dip in the waters.

Although bathing in the Dead Sea is perfectly safe and the water

is always accessible, one is strongly advised only to swim at properly equipped bathing places, which have changing facilities and showers or fresh-water pools for washing. The salt water leaves the skin unpleasantly sticky when it dries. Kallia has recently been equipped with these necessities.

This part of the Desert of Judea, with its many networks of caves, has been one of the richest areas for important archaeological discoveries, including letters and documents as well as more substantial artefacts. Certainly the most sensational discovery was that of what are known as the Dead Sea Scrolls, which were found at Qumran, the first site at which the visitor must pause on his tour of the Dead Sea.

the site can be seen remains of its fortifications, the ritual immersion baths and – as we frequently find in these sophisticated desert settlements – elaborate systems for catching water. The most interesting room discovered when Qumran was excavated in the 1950s was the scriptorium (or writing room) where, it is assumed, the scrolls were written. In it there was a smooth-topped writing desk and inkwells. The cave where the scrolls were found may also be viewed, as well as kitchens, stables and cemetery.

The other celebrated and unmissable landmark on the Dead Sea is the dramatic fortress of Masada, but on the way there are several enticements to pause a while.

Every few miles natural, fresh-water springs pour down the bleak

These pages: Bethlehem, an enchanting town of spires and steeples whose name resounds throughout the world as the birthplace of Christ. The Church of the Nativity (right) stands over and around the Grotto, or Chapel of the Nativity (overleaf). Here, beneath a small altar, a Silver Star marks the spot where it is thought that Jesus was born.

Every guidebook reports how the scrolls were discovered accidentally in 1947 by a young Bedouin shepherd hunting a lost goat in the barren cliffs. The scrolls include the oldest manuscripts of the Old Testament. Scientific evidence indicates that they were written about 100 BC and they bear a close similarity to Hebrew texts still used today. They are now housed in a specially-designed building as part of the Israel Museum in Jerusalem.

At Qumran today can be seen the remains of the ancient Jewish community called the Essenes, in whose archives the scrolls rested. The Essenes were a breakaway sect preferring a remote, almost monastic existence in the desert to the demands (and possibly temptations) of city life. They were finally annihilated by the Romans in AD 68, but not before they had hidden their archives in the nearby caves, where they rested undisturbed and unseen for so many centuries.

Qumran is high and commands splendid views in all directions. At

hillsides to the Dead Sea, creating a series of oases rich in plantlife, trees, wild animals and sweet water pools which are perfect for taking a quick dip before venturing into the sea – and perhaps a more leisurely one afterwards.

Travelling south from Qumran, the first oasis is Ein Fashcha, which is a nature reserve. There is a tree-shaded canal, pools and facilities for bathing and refreshments. It is, in fact, an extremely popular spot for the locals, especially at weekends when it can be as crowded as any of the Mediterranean beaches: people bring their cars, tents, parasols and picnics; children play and both the sea and the pools are packed.

A few miles further on is the Kibbutz Mitzpe Shalem, and on the way the road rises to afford spectacular views of the sea, the moon-like landscape and particularly the gorge of Nahal Dragot.

And then another oasis is found. This time it is one of the most famous of all: Ein Gedi (Fountain of the Kid). It is primarily famous because it is specifically mentioned in the Bible as the place where David hid from the wrath of Saul, and there are references to it in the psalms suggesting that even then it was famous for its luxuriant

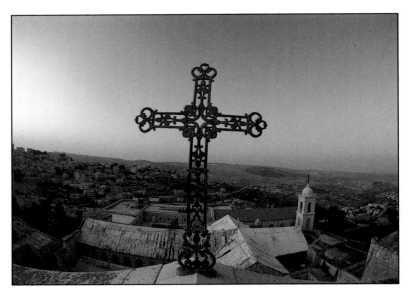

These pages: scenes from Bethlehem, where Hagop Avakian carves holy figures in olive wood (left and above left). Top: a view from the roof of the Church of the Nativity, (facing page) an olive tree and (above) a bas-relief sculpture on the gate to the Milk Grotto, where tradition maintains that Mary spilt milk while nursing Jesus and the drops turned the black stones a milky white.

flowers and foliage. In Roman times it was famous for its dates.

And it is today. The splendid stand of date palms, cultivated by the Kibbutz Ein Gedi, makes a handsome sight against the barren hills. In the date grove is the mosaic floor of an ancient synagogue and nearby are the remains of a Chalcolithic temple. This area is one of Israel's best-known nature reserves – Nahal David – which includes trails through luscious vegetation and beside small waterfalls. There is a mountain pool, and ibex, wild goats and rare birds are easily seen. There are also leopards, but they keep well away from people and present no threat to the visitor.

A few miles south of Ein Gedi is the huge, lumpish mountain called Masada. In this particular terrain of jagged, flat-topped hills, dizzy precipices and vast gorges, Masada seems little different from any other outcrop. However, its history and its significance have a

Top: a Christmas procession in Bethlehem (these pages), (above and top right) the Silver Star in the Chapel of the Nativity, under the beautiful Basilica of the Nativity (facing page top), which was originally built at the time of Constantine. Right: the spires of the holy town rising up into the dawn sky.

central, symbolic power for Israel; its story has been described as 'part of the Israeli national experience'.

Masada is the Hebrew word for fortress, which is what the mountain was. It's flat, boat-shaped top – extremely difficult of access from the ground – suggests an ideal site for a stronghold, and it was first developed as such by Herod the Great in the first century BC. He designed it as a retreat for his household should his discontented subjects revolt, or in case he was attacked by Cleopatra. After his death it fell into the hands of the Romans, who maintained it as a small outpost.

In AD 66 open Jewish revolt broke out against Rome, Jewish zealots overpowered the Romans at Masada and it became an

Top and above: views of Jerusalem, the capital of Israel and a holy city for Christians, Jews and Muslims, dominated by the Dome of the Rock (right) in the Temple Area (facing page). This beautiful octagonal mosque crowns the Sacred Rock that is believed by both Muslims and Jews to be the foundation stone of the world.

armed Jewish camp. Four years later Jerusalem fell and survivors joined the group at Masada, which held out alone against Rome until AD 72, when the 10th Roman Legion set out to crush finally this last point of resistance.

The zealots held out against a dedicated siege, but finally, when it became clear that the Roman commander had found a way of storming the fortress, the zealots committed mass suicide in order to prevent capture and enslavement. When the Romans finally reached the summit it was abundantly clear that the Jewish rebels were not short of supplies or ammunition.

The story of Masada was first recorded by the Jewish historian

Josephus Flavius (who joined the Romans at the time), and scholars had always considered the tale to be fictitious, or at least elaborated. However, Masada was finally excavated between 1963 and 1965 under the lead of Professor Yigael Yadin with the help of the Israeli army and thousands of volunteers from some 28 countries.

Flavius' account makes for extraordinarily moving reading, and now that its authenticity is established, it is little wonder that Masada has become such a potent symbol. Many Israeli tank corps hold their swearing-in ceremonies on the summit, and Bar Mitzvah ceremonies are also held there.

Masada has been thoroughly excavated, its various rooms, tunnels, baths and store rooms identified and its various periods of occupation ascertained. It was found, for example, that its final occupants had been a group of 5th century Byzantine monks. A visit to Masada is essential for any visitor to Israel and it is worth setting aside a day to study it properly. Knowledge of the background saga makes the tour a potent experience.

Intrepid or determined visitors will want to gain the summit by using the snake path which winds laboriously up the eastern face of

the cliff. Amazingly this path, used by the zealots, was kept a secret not only from the Romans but also through the following centuries. It used to be dangerous, but is not so now – just very hard work indeed.

In 1970 a cablecar was installed, so now there is an effortless way of reaching Masada's relics. The vertical ascent is more than 1,000 feet from the base of the mountain. There are plenty of water points installed, and visitors should be sure to wear sunhats. From the summit of Masada the view of desert and sea is spectacular, and also clearly visible is the outline of the Roman camp far below.

The excavations revealed that Herod the Great did not simply build himself a practical fortress, but a luxurious palace as well. At the northern end of the plateau are the living quarters, hanging in three tiers one below the other down the side of the mountain.

The upper terrace contained domestic quarters, but the lower ones seem to have been designed mainly for pleasure, paved as they are with mosaics and supported by lines of slender, elegant columns. The middle terrace is circular and, of course, there are splendid views from all of them. Herod also built another palace

which he retained for public events. Masada also has a remarkably luxurious bathing complex with a changing room, cold room, tepid room and a large hot room ingeniously heated. There are numerous storehouses, temples and an impressive water system which would not only supply the garrison's basic needs but also the luxuries of baths and swimming pools. Relics of the Jewish occupancy include a 'mikve' or ritual bath, ingeniously adapted from Herod's scheme, as well as some touching personal objects. There is also a structure believed to be a synagogue which would make it the oldest synagogue yet discovered. Sacred scrolls were also discovered here.

The scheme that the Romans devised to storm Masada involved the building of a massive earth ramp up against the lowest side of the mountain. Jewish captives were set to work on it, and the final assault was launched with mobile siege tower, catapults and a battering ram. The ramp can still be seen, plus piles of hundreds of rounded stones about the size of grapefruit, which poured from the catapults.

There are other sights in Israel, other buildings, which are more obviously glamorous and eye-catching than Masada, but none pulls the visitor so deeply into the country's turbulent history or brings a sense of the distant past so vividly to life.

Facing page: (top) Montefiore's Windmill in Yemin Moshe, the first Jewish Quarter built outside Jerusalem's Old City (bottom). Below: the Garden Tomb, believed by some to be the Tomb of Joseph of Arimathea where Christ's body was laid after the Crucifixion, (bottom left) the tombs of Zachariah and St James and (bottom right) Dormition Abbey on Mt Zion.

Eating

A table, laden with food, seemed to stretch endlessly along one wall

of the dining room. Guests wandered in, approached and just gazed open-mouthed at the display. There were eggs, boiled or scrambled, a huge variety of salads fresh and gleaming, aubergine dips, houmus, huge tomatoes, cucumbers, bowls of olives, pickled herrings, a variety of cheeses, yoghurt with chopped peppers, yoghurt with chopped apricots, a wide range of breads including sweet ones, orange juice and coffee.

Israel may have no national cuisine, but it has a national culinary institution – breakfast. The breakfast buffet just described was offered in a good hotel in central Jerusalem, but you will find something very similar wherever you go, whether in a private house or on a kibbutz. The range may be smaller in less expensive hotels, but the same main ingredients will be there – breads, yoghurt, startlingly fresh salads and fruit, and always orange juice.

This is probably the healthiest food in the western world – nourishing, sustaining and definitely not weight-producing. And the traveller will soon discover that a hearty breakfast along these lines will sustain him through the day with, perhaps, a snack around lunchtime.

Otherwise, the country offers no consistent kind of cooking which could definitely be labelled Israeli. Instead there is the most extraordinary range of cooking derived from all over the world, from

Above left: a full moon over Jerusalem (these pages). Top left: praying at the Wailing Wall, which is customary for Jews on holy days and at important times in an individual's life, (left) a concert in the Citadel and (above) the Rockefeller Museum. Facing page: (top) the ancient walls of Jerusalem and (bottom) the stone arch of the 'Hurvah' Synagogue.

all the countries, in fact, that Jewish people have come from. So one can find Chinese, Argentinian, Italian and middle-European food.

All these different cuisines do, however, have one thing in common – they conform to the Jewish dietary laws (called 'keeping Kosher'). Apart from the ban on pork and certain shellfish this basically means that dairy products and meat are not served at the same meal. Although all of Israel's hotels are kosher, not all its restaurants are, especially those in the big towns and cities on the Mediterranean coast, where shellfish are so fresh and so good.

First-time visitors – especially from Europe and America – tend to expect Israeli food to be like the Jewish food common in the West. Of course, immigrants have established these great specialities, but Israel is essentially a middle-eastern country and the food of the eastern Mediterranean basin has the greatest influence: among the basics that Israel has certainly made its own are felafel, houmus and pitta bread. This makes the perfect mid-day snack, eaten at leisure at a café table or munched while wandering along.

Israel's own produce features widely, of course, including the fine citrus fruit, tomatoes, avocados, celery and green salad vegetables.

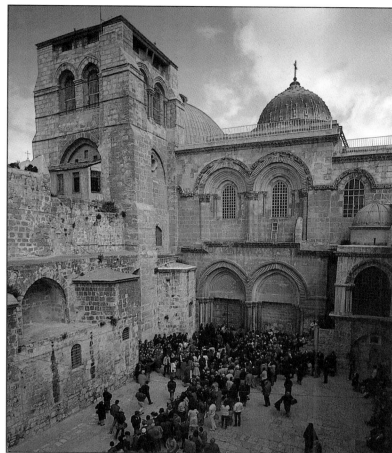

Facing page: rooftops in Jerusalem's Christian Quarter, (top) Mea She'arim, the ultra-Orthodox Jewish Quarter, (top right) the Easter procession in front of the Church of the Holy Sepulchre, which marks the site of the Crucifixion and is considered by many to be the holiest of Christian shrines, (above right) the 'Hurvah' Synagogue and (above) the old Jewish cemetery on the Mount of Olives.

The Arab influence is there with kebabs and with piles of rich, tempting cakes and pastries gleaming from stalls in the souks and street markets of the big towns. Freshly pressed orange and grapefruit juice is always available – and (along with the ubiquitous hunks of water melon) very welcome as a refresher when exploring the hot and dusty byways of the ancient cities.

The West Bank: Bethlehem, Jerusalem and Surrounds

Many visitors to Israel confess themselves unsure as to what is actually meant by the definition 'West Bank'. It is, in fact, a political designation and refers to that part of the British Mandate of Palestine west of the River Jordan. It was occupied by Jordan until the Six Day War of 1967 and has remained under Israeli control ever since.

Jericho and the Jordan Rift valley are also part of the West Bank, but predominantly the term is used to refer to Judaea and Samaria (the preferred names used by the Israelis themselves), which constitute what we call the Holy Land. Jerusalem is the centre and around this city are the areas in which so many of the events recorded in the Bible happened.

Judaea lies to the south of Jerusalem and includes Bethlehem which is, of course, a town of some significance in both the Old and

New testaments, and also Hebron, where Abraham was buried. It is in this area that the visitor is most likely to sense a biblical atmosphere; there are villages and farms shaded by olive groves, and ox-drawn ploughs can still be seen. And the wilderness of Judaea, stretching towards the Dead Sea, casts the spell of the desert.

Samaria, to the north of Jerusalem, shows a different face. The countryside is greener and lusher, with pines and other trees – evidence of afforestation projects. The town of Ramallah is one of the most beautiful, prosperous and elegant, but the largest and most important city is Nablus (Shechem in the Bible) and remains the principal centre of the Samaritans.

The West Bank is, then, the biblical heartland of Israel, where every building, almost every stone, well and pathway is full of

Facing page: inside the magnificent Dome of the Rock (above), which was built in AD 691 and stands on the site of the Temple of Solomon, over the rock upon which Adam was made, Cain slew Abel, Abraham prepared to sacrifice Isaac and from which Mohammed ascended to heaven.

resonance. But it would be a mistake to expect to find an air of holy reverence hovering about these towns. They are bustling, busy places with sometimes heavy traffic and thriving industrial sections. But the holy sites, the churches and shrines, are beautifully kept and, when not too crowded, can project a feeling of peace and quiet.

In Hebrew, the word Bethlehem means 'House of Bread'. In the Old Testament it is recorded as the place where Ruth and Boaz fell

in love, and is noted as the birthplace of King David. Rachel, wife of Jacob, was, according to the Bible, buried here, and a domed building (built in 1841) commemorates her. It is a focus for Jewish pilgrims, and Rachel's tomb is also revered in Islam, so there is a Muslim cemetery there, too. As so often in Israel, one finds that a single place carries importance for the three great religions.

Of Bethlehem's population of 25,000, just more than half are Muslim, the rest Christian Arabs.

Bethlehem does retain a great deal of atmosphere for, as the place where Christ was born, it has been a focus of pilgrimage and reverence for centuries. The town has survived earthquakes and wars and today is a peaceful place, its skyline punctuated with spires and steeples, its alleys and streets yielding many different Christian shrines, its periphery pastoral with vineyards and olive groves.

Eventually, everyone makes for Manger Square where the Basilica of the Nativity stands. Fortress-like from the outside, somewhat austere inside, the church was originally built in the 4th century but largely re-built 600 years later. The entrance in unusually low, deliberately built so as to prevent anyone with sacrilegious intent from riding in on horseback. The two rows of columns inside date

Facing page bottom: the Easter procession near the Holy Sepulchre Church, where Franciscans celebrate Mass (facing page top) and Greek Orthodox nuns pray (top). Above left: celebrating the Sukkoth, a Jewish harvest festival commemorating the 40 years in the desert, (above) the sounding of the shofar, a musical instrument made from a ram's horn, and (left) Mea She'arim, in the Jewish Quarter.

from the 6th century, which makes this the oldest church in Israel.

Stairways on either side of the main altar lead down to the Grotto of the Nativity immediately beneath. A silver star marks the spot where Christ was born, seventeen lamps burn constantly and the scent of incense hangs heavily in the air. The grotto, like the church itself, is under the jurisdiction of the Greek Orthodox Church; the Roman Catholic church of St Catherine is next door and linked to the main church. It is in St Catherine's that the traditional midnight mass is celebrated on Christmas Eve each year. The church also contains grottoes commemorating St Joseph, St Jerome and the Massacre of the Innocents.

In fact Christmas is celebrated three times in Bethlehem. The Western Christian festivities happen first; the Greek Orthodox observation is on January 7, while the Armenians celebrate on January 19th. Each one has its own processions, bands and singers, and they all happen in Manger Square. But in the summer, too, this square has colourful attractions with its mix of multinational tourists, religious people in different robes and gowns, women from the outlying villages in traditional dress, busy cafés and restaurants.

Other sites worth seeing in Bethlehem include David's Wells, three large cisterns where King David is said to have 'longed to drink' when Bethlehem was held by the Philistines, and the Milk Grotto, where tradition says that the Virgin Mary spilled some of her milk, turning the black stones of the grotto to a milky white. Little packets of the powdered, white stone are sold to pilgrims, and it is alleged to increase the flow of mothers' milk.

Naturally, Bethlehem has its souk, which possesses all the

Facing page: (top) the Jaffa Gate and (bottom) the Damascus Gate, both leading through the Old City walls into the Christian Quarter. Top: a Palm Sunday procession descends the Mount of Olives, site of the beautiful Garden of Gethsemane (above). Here, marking the place of Christ's Agony, stands the Church of All Nations (left), overlooked by the Russian Church of St Mary Magdalene.

flavour and colour of the Orient, with Arabs in their striking robes and a great variety of leather and brassware as well as fruit and vegetables.

A few kilometres south of Bethlehem lies Herodion which, like Masada, is a desert fortress-palace built by King Herod. It is a symmetrical, flat-topped cone created by cutting off the top of a hill and adjusting the sides into symmetry – quite a feat for the king's architects and builders.

The impressive monument stands 758 metres (2,464 feet) above sea level and the towers were raised over 33 metres (70 feet) from the floor of the fortress. It commands stunning views over the Desert of Judaea and the Dead Sea on one side, and over the hills to the outskirts of Jerusalem on the other. Herod is alleged to have been buried here, but no tomb has been found. Remains include stone

benches and a ritual bath.

Penetrating further and higher into the Judaean mountains we come to Hebron, a city particularly holy to Jews and also venerated by Muslims as the burial place of the Patriarchs. The city has had a turbulent history, reaching a climax in 1929 when some 60 Jews were killed during Arab rioting.

The main feature of interest here is the Cave of Machpela, which Abraham bought as a burial site for his wife Sarah. They are buried here along with Isaac and Jacob and their wives Rebecca and Leah. The tombs themselves are said to be deep in a cave below the monument which was built over them by Herod with stones very similar to those used for the Western Wall in Jerusalem, which he also built. There is a lavishly-decorated mosque nearby.

Hebron has its network of alleyways and interesting streets and courtyards, and its souk. A speciality is glass-blowing (believed to have been introduced from Venice by Jewish immigrants after the Crusades), and one can watch objects being made over open fires, using ancient methods.

The religious, historical, emotional and spiritual reverberations of Jerusalem are powerful. For thousands of years the city was regarded as the centre of the world, not just geographically (seeming to form the central junction of Europe, Asia and Africa), but spiritually, too. It is a city of equal importance to Christians, Jews and Muslims, containing within its periphery shrines and sites sacred and fundamental to each of the great religions.

Politically divided for so many years, the city's reunification in 1967 prompted an outburst of development and growth, with tower blocks, modern, imaginatively-designed public buildings, road systems and commercial centres befitting its role as the capital of the modern state of Israel.

It is, therefore, a city of great contrasts. One moment one could be in any developed city of the west, yet the next moment, simply by turning a corner, the atmosphere is as peaceful and ancient as if it had lain undisturbed for centuries. There are small neighbourhoods developed in the 19th century and across the road the hurly-burly glamour of the Arabian Nights. Café society – night and day – flourishes in the modern city, while behind the massive walls of the Old City life seems to have continued unchanged since the days of Herod.

Yet Jerusalem has none of the slightly raffish quality of Tel Aviv and some of the coastal centres. It remains essentially a serious city; there's a smile on its face and warmth in its heart, but it is also decorous and grave.

Archaeological documentation suggests that Jerusalem is 5,000 years old and the oldest of the world's continuously-inhabited cities. David made it the capital of the kingdom of a united Israel in 1000 BC and Solomon built the Temple. Both the city and the Temple were destroyed many times, only to be rebuilt again and again, and one estimate has it that Jerusalem has survived something like 30 or more conquests. From the 12th century to the present century, however, the city held no particular significance politically, and it wasn't until 1917, when the British Army under General Allenby entered the Holy City, that it began to assume international importance.

Above: Yad Vashem – memorial to the 6,000,000 victims of the Holocaust, on Mount Herzl, Jerusalem. Left: Hebrew University, Mount Scopus, Jerusalem. Facing page: Dizengoff Centre (top left), Tel Aviv. Tourists and residents (top right) in downtown Tel Aviv, and customers browsing (bottom) in Steimatzky's, Israel's leading bookstore chain.

Jerusalem contains, therefore, an amazing array of buildings, relics, churches and other significant locations which make the Bible spring to life (some even suggest taking a Bible as guide-book!), and also many of the glories of modern Israel.

Where the visitor might begin to tackle this jewel box of delights could be a problem. But before exploring individual sights, it might be a good idea to take a walk of orientation in the way first-time visitors to Amsterdam enjoy a canal tour, or to New York take the round-the-island boat trip. In Jerusalem this means strolling along the ramparts of the walls of the Old City. This gives one some indication of the scale of the city and its layout, for the views of the city and its surrounding hills are quite spectacular. Only one short section of the

wall is not open to the public, and another is broken by one of the city gates.

The Old City's handsome stone wall was built by the Suleimen the magnificent in the 16th century and is 4km (2.5 miles) long. There are eight gates, and within lie several major focal points for the visitor: the great Dome of the Rock, the Via Dolorosa, the Church of the Holy Sepulchre and, of course, the Wailing Wall, which is part of the massive wall Herod built to contain the Second Temple.

From the ramparts one can see the high-rise blocks of West Jerusalem, the Mount of Olives, Mount Scopus and the beginning of the desert of Judaea. But perhaps even more fascinating is the view looking *inside* the Old City. The chief landmarks, which stand above

Facing page: (top) the newly-built Ramat Eshcol suburb, and (bottom) a view from the Mount of Olives with the Church of the Ascension in the foreground and modern Jerusalem (top right) on the horizon. Above: the Menorah, the seven-branched candelabrum that symbolises the independence of Israel and stands opposite the Knesset building (top). Right: the Jewish Quarter.

the rest of the buildings and are immediately recognisable, are the golden dome of the Dome of the Rock and the Tower of David. But between them lie some 220 acres (about one square kilometre) of packed rooftops, minarets, domes, walls, flat roofs and churches, hiding a seething, crowded, colourful Oriental town. Some roofs are made of ancient tiles, others are patched with tarpaulin or improvised with sheets of corrugated iron; lines of washing are strung across many and each sports its television aeriel. Arabs in their flowing robes, tourists, donkeys, chickens, children, severely-dressed religious Jews Hend ordinary housewives throng the narrow streets, alleys and exotic bazaars. The *muezzin's* call to prayer (electronically amplified these days) resounds from the minarets, while below pop music shrieks from transistor radios carried by teenagers.

Any visitor entering the Old City through the Jaffa Gate can be forgiven if he temporarily forgets about the religious sites as the hustle, excitement and scented glamour of the souk arrests his attention. The narrow streets meet in arches overhead, and dark passages are suddenly illuminated by shafts of brilliant sunlight. Stalls and open shops stand cheek by jowl selling everything from leather and brassware to clothes, spices and vegetables. There are

Bottom: Yemenite Jews and (below) a Jewish family observing the ritual Seder meal at the start of the Passover, which involves the recitation of Exodus. Right: a Yemenite scribe correcting a Torah scroll and (facing page) Hasidic Jewish children at their 'cheder', or Bible school. Overleaf: the Temple Area in the heart of Jerusalem.

Facing page: the Citadel, the great fort first built by Herod the Great in 24 BC, and (above) the Shrine of the Book in the grounds of the Israel Museum, Jerusalem. Overleaf: the Wailing Wall and the Dome of Rock.

mouth-watering cake and sweet stalls, the rich pastries neatly piled up in pyramids and displayed against mirrored walls, making them seem even more plentiful and luxurious than they are. Souvenirs, ornaments and bric-a-brac abound. If you haven't already got one, this is the place to buy a straw sunhat – essential protection in this country.

The Jaffa Gate (so called because the road from here leads directly to Jaffa on the coast) is built at an angle to prevent any direct attack. When General Allenby entered the City as its conqueror in 1917 he tactfully insisted that he and his staff should dismount from their horses and enter on foot. Just inside the gate is the Citadel, a huge, 2,000-year-old tower built by Herod the Great. The Tower of David is here too, but, like the gate itself, it is 16th-century and Turkish.

Archaeological digs are always underway. The courtyard of the Citadel has been thoroughly excavated, revealing layers of many different periods. All this can be seen in detail, well-documented, in

the attached museum.

The Old City has its various, well-defined quarters – Armenian, Jewish, Christian and Muslim. Each has its own character and the Jewish one is particularly interesting since it was severely damaged in the 1948 fighting, abandoned, and then lay untouched for a generation. Restoration began in 1967. The opportunity was taken to carry out excavations which resulted in the discovery of some important sites. These include a series of Crusader-period archways, a section of the old city wall dating back to 701 BC and the remains of a house which had burned in the Roman sacking of AD

Right: a synagogue's window displays, in vividly-coloured stained glass, an image of the Menorah, which burnt before the Ark in the Temple at Jerusalem. Below: praying at the Wailing Wall, (bottom) Hass Promenade, Talpiot, looking towards Jerusalem from the south, and (facing page) the Russian Church of St Mary Magdalene, Jerusalem.

70. The new buildings that have been put up since then harmonise with their surroundings – the archways, for example, are incorporated into a row of modern shops. The whole area has a unique charm of its own.

Facing page: (top) Israeli flags fly before the plaza of the Western, or Wailing Wall, and (bottom) the Christian symbols of chalice and thorns adorn a window in the Dominus Flevit Church. Below: the Citadel, (bottom right) leaving the Old City of Jerusalem through the Zion Gate, and (bottom) the Mount of Olives, topped by the Church of the Ascension rising beyond the silver dome of the El Aksa Mosque.

From the Jewish Quarter steps lead down to a wide, open space and one is confronted by the Wailing, or Western Wall. This is not, as is often popularly thought, an actual part of the Jewish Second Temple. It was built some 2,000 years ago as a retaining wall for the temple itself; the Wailing Wall is the western end of this. When the Second Temple was destroyed by the Romans, Jews were forbidden the area for so long that the actual location of the temple itself was forgotten. Eventually this one segment of wall was seen as the nearest they could get to the sacred area without actually entering it. Here they mourned the destruction of the Temple – hence 'Wailing Wall'. Another interpretation of the name derives from the fact that dew forms on the stones in the early morning, making it seems as if the wall itself is weeping.

This is an important place for prayer and religious observances,

and it functions according to the rules of an orthodox synagogue, with male and female worshippers segregated. There are no formal services; people come to pray alone or in groups, sometimes many at the same time (especially on the Sabbath). Bar Mitzvah services take place at the Wall, and when Sabbath begins (Friday evenings) the area is crowded.

Despite the profound significance of the Wall, during the day the atmosphere tends to be light and relaxed. Lines of men – some soberly-suited, others in short sleeves – sit close to the wall, praying and perhaps leaving a prayer or plea pushed between the great

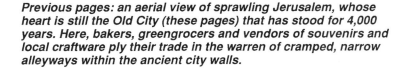

Previous pages: an aerial view of sprawling Jerusalem, whose heart is still the Old City (these pages) that has stood for 4,000 years. Here, bakers, greengrocers and vendors of souvenirs and local craftware ply their trade in the warren of cramped, narrow alleyways within the ancient city walls.

stones. But they are undisturbed by the colourful crowds of tourists and the distant rattle of the surrounding city. To feel some of the deeper reverberations of the place, a visit at a quiet time – perhaps in the early evening or at night (the wall is accessible all the time) is the best idea.

This wall originally formed the base of the Temple Mount – and it is interesting to note that 20 metres of it lie below ground level. The vast rectangular area (some 40 acres) enclosed by the wall was filled in by Herod, and on this he built the Temple. Today, this feat of building remains impressive, consisting of a broad, paved square with elegant kiosks and dotted with cypress trees. It is dominated by

the Dome of the Rock which is one of Jerusalem's most arresting sights.

There really is a naked outcrop of rock under that great golden dome – some traditions claim it as the centre of the world. It is, in fact, the summit of Mount Moriah which, since the name is mentioned in Genesis, has led it to be regarded as the site of Abraham's preparations to sacrifice his son Isaac. When Solomon raised his magnificent temple he incorporated the rock into it. Later, the second temple was also built on this site but was later destroyed without trace.

When the Arab caliph, Omar Ibn-Khatib, wanted to build a mosque in the newly-conquered Jerusalem he had to remove layers of rubbish to reveal the rock. Muslim tradition states that it was from this rock that Mohammed rose to heaven – a mark on the already pitted and earthquake-cracked surface of the rock is pointed out today as his horse's footprint. Be that as it may, the raw rock is an impressive sight surrounded as it is by an exquisitely-beautiful piece of architecture.

The Dome of the Rock (its correct name and not the Mosque of

Omar as one sometimes hears) was built in AD 691 by the caliph Abd el-Malik. Inside and out, the octagonal building is beautifully decorated and in most respects is just as it was 13 centuries ago. Elaborate and exquisitely-worked mosaics cover most surfaces, many of them original. The marble work (which includes the two circles of pillars) inside the building dates from the 12th century, and the glazed tiles on the exterior were added by Suleiman the Magnificent in the 16th century.

It is believed that the original dome was made from real gold, but this was later removed and replaced by lead. The most recent renovations to the building were made in 1963 and included replacing the dome yet again, this time with bronze-aluminium. Many would like to see it replaced by the original gilded wood and there is a possibility that this might happen.

Muslim law forbids the representation of humans or animals in decorative motifs, so all the designs are either pure geometry or

From the pale stone city of Jerusalem (these pages) rise the gleaming domes of the Dome of the Rock (above), the silver El Aksa Mosque (facing page bottom) and the Russian Church of St Mary Magdalene (left), built in the late 1800s by Czar Alexander III. Facing page top: the 6th-century Monastery of the Cross, which is thought to mark the site of the tree from which Christ's cross was made.

floral, with grapes and ears of corn, as well as quotations from the Koran, written in elaborate Arab script. Beside the rock itself stands a tall casket which contains hairs believed to be from the Prophet Mohammed's beard, and below the rock is a cave known as the Well of Souls.

Nearby, at the southern end of the Mount of the Temple, stands the El Aqsa Mosque with its dark grey dome. This was built some 20 years after the Dome of the Rock, but has suffered more through the years, mainly from earthquakes since, not having been built on solid rock, it was more vulnerable to shocks. A cursory examination of the interior reveals the different kinds of reconstruction work that have been carried out over the years, and this is the fourth building on this site.

Built right up against the southern wall of the Temple Mount, it is a cavernous, slightly gloomy building, a forest of columns (there are three aisles each side of the central nave) but with some beautiful stained glass windows which add a little colour. These were added in the 16th century. 'El Aqsa' means 'the distant place' – from Mecca, that is.

There are one or two grim contemporary memories in this mosque as well. In 1951, King Abdullah of the Transjordan was assassinated here – a bullet mark on the pillar near the entrance is

and elegance pervading the whole of the plateau.

Jerusalem's Old City is so packed with places of great significance for adherents of all three great religions that it is, of course, always packed with pilgrims, for some of whom the visit is the climax of a lifetime of hope and ambition.

One item on every itinerary is to trace the Stations of the Cross along the Via Dolorosa. This is the route which is believed to have been taken by Jesus when forced to carry his cross from the place of his trial to that of his execution and burial. The 14 stations mark incidents, some mentioned in the Gospels, and some additional traditions.

The route begins in the Muslim quarter of the Old City and winds along narrow streets and under arches, one of which was a triumphal

Facing page: (bottom) the walls of the Old City by the Jaffa Gate (top). Below: the Russian Church of St Mary Magdalene, and (left) the Basilica of the Agony in the Garden of Gethsemane, also known as the Church of All Nations as each of its twelve shallow domes contains a mosaic donated by a different country.

a reminder. In 1969 a fire was deliberately started and a priceless medieval ebony pulpit was destroyed.

Muslims pray at the El Aqsa Mosque five times a day, and also at the Dome of the Rock, but individually rather than communally. Visitors are asked to dress modestly when visiting the shrines (head, arms and legs covered – no shorts for men or women), and must leave their shoes, bags and cameras outside.

On the terrace between the two splendidly-domed mosques is the Fountain of the Cup (El Kas), fed by water from subterranean cisterns, and used by many Muslims for washing their feet before entering the holy buildings.

On four sides of the Dome of the Rock, and some distance from it, stand slender, arched, stone screens which add to the air of grace

arch built by the Emperor Hadrian a century after Christ. Each Station of the Cross is marked on the pavement by a semi-circle of cobblestones. A Franciscan procession moves along the Via Dolorosa every Friday afternoon, and pilgrims may join it.

It is believed that the site of Pontius Pilate's Judgement Hall was later occupied by a fortress named after Mark Antony by Herod and is now a school. This is the first Station. Opposite is the Monastery of the Flagellation where Christ was whipped and given the cross – Station II. The third marks the place where Jesus fell beneath the weight of the cross. A chapel built by Free Polish soldiers after the Second World War marks this. Next is the place where Mary came out of the crowd to greet her son (Station IV), and a little further on a chapel is dedicated to St Simon of Cyrene who was ordered by the

Above: Franciscan monks in the Palm Sunday procession (left) on the Mount of Olives. Since the Crusader era, the Franciscan Order has been the Catholic Church's main representative in Jerusalem and is thought to have been founded there following St Francis's visit in 1219. Among their churches is Dominus Flevit, through the main window of which can be seen the Dome of the Rock (facing page).

Romans to help carry the cross (Station V).

The Via Dolorosa takes a double bend here and the pilgrim begins to climb a steeper street. Halfway up is the Church of St Veronica, recalling that a woman stepped up to Jesus and wiped his face, his image being imprinted on the cloth. The name associated with this incident – Veronica – is derived from the Latin *vera icone* – 'true image'. This is Station VI. At the top of the hill is Station VII where Christ fell for a second time. Two Franciscan chapels stand here.

The next station (VIII) is just off the main street, where a cross on the wall of a Greek Orthodox monastery marks the place where Jesus addressed the women of Jerusalem. Station IX is the spot where Jesus fell for the third time and is marked by a pillar at the door of a Coptic convent. This is very close to the Church of the Holy Sepulchre, and it is within this church that the last of the fourteen stations are located.

If the Dome of the Rock and the Wailing Wall are among the holiest shrines of the Muslim and Jewish faiths respectively, then the Church of the Holy Sepulchre is one of the holiest for Christians, who revere it as the site of the death, burial and resurrection of Christ. The present building seems to be a conglomeration of different edifices, with a square, almost European-style tower and two large domes, while the houses of the Old City crowd closely up to it. A succession of much larger Byzantine churches have stood on this site; the church we see today was rebuilt by Crusaders in the 12th century. They built the bell tower and the facade, which has two fine stonework arches over the entrance.

Inside the Catholic Chapel are Stations X (Jesus is stripped of his clothes) and XI (He is nailed to the cross). In the Greek Orthodox Chapel is Station XII – Jesus dies on the cross. Beneath the altar is a bronze disc marking the actual spot where the cross is believed to

have stood. Station XIII is where the body was taken down. Opposite the entrance to the church is the Stone of Unction, a slab on which, it is said, the body was washed and prepared for burial.

The Gospel story relates that Christ's body was buried in a rock tomb in a nearby garden. Today, a large marble slab beneath the great rotunda covers the tomb – Station XIV.

The church – in which so many denominations are present – is richly decorated and religious ceremonies are constantly taking place amid an atmosphere created by candles, chanting and the heavy scent of incense. There are some excellent mosaics, statues and hanging lamps, which make the place mysterious and exotic as well as being a place of reverent worship.

To itemise every sight in the Old City would require a complete guide book (and there are plenty available), but these are the major items which any visitor on a tight schedule should make a priority. There is so much to interest, fascinate and draw the attention among the bustling alleys that many people find themselves returning again and again. There are eight gates into the city, some of which are blocked now, and we have already looked at the Jaffa Gate and its nearby Citadel. The Damascus Gate in the northern stretch of the wall is the largest and most impressive of the gates, and is also the main thoroughfare between the Old City and the Arab quarters of East Jerusalem. Its layered arches and crennellations (it was built in 1538, though Herod is understood to have created a gate here as well) lend it a sense of ceremony and importance.

Outside the walls, a comfortable pedestrian parade, lined with palm trees and affording good views over the newer parts of Jerusalem, links the Jaffa and Damascus gates.

To the south and east of the Old City lie two of the many significant hills on which Jerusalem is built – Mount Zion and the Mount of Olives.

Right: the Lithostratos, the Roman paving stones below Jerusalem's Ecce Homo Convent of the Sisters of Zion, upon which Christ was tried and mocked, and (below) a bas-relief at the 4th Station of the Cross in an oratory by the Church of Our Lady of the Spasm. Facing page: (top) the Israel Museum's Shrine of the Book, which houses the Dead Sea Scrolls, and (bottom) the Byzantine Cardo Street excavations in the Old City's Jewish Quarter.

The name 'Zion' is synonymous with Jerusalem itself and the hill is a continuation of the plateau of the Old City, to the south, with no valley separating it. The main point of interest here is King David's Tomb, a large stone memorial which, for centuries, has been the

focus of countless pilgrims. Above the tomb is the Cenacle – or Room of the Last Supper, which was built in the 12th century and was later used as a mosque.

Next door is the Benedictine Dormition Abbey (where Mary 'fell into eternal sleep'). Built at the beginning of this century, it is a striking building and something of a landmark on Mount Zion, with its conical-roofed tower and tall clock tower. Apparently, the original idea was to create a much larger complex of buildings, incorporating the Tomb of David, but this failed to materialise. Also on Mount Zion are the Chamber of the Holocaust and the Church of St Peter at Cockcrow.

The Mount of Olives is steep, but the climb is worthwhile because from the summit one gets a spectacular view of Jerusalem,

Facing page: (bottom) the Knesset Building, and (top) spring blossoms framing a view of the Dome of the Rock (this page bottom) Below: the white dome of the Shrine of the Book contrasting with the black slab that symbolises darkness, and (bottom right) the Kennedy Memorial, which, in the form of a truncated tree, denotes a life cut short.

particularly of the Old City. The Mount's fame is so great that it is a prime target for visitors and pilgrims and is consequently also a prime target for souvenir-sellers, camel-drivers and postcard stalls.

Never mind – some of the goods on sale, especially the olive-wood carvings and small statues, are worth looking at seriously. Most of the rising slopes of the Mount of Olives consist of the most ancient and revered Jewish cemetery, believed to be the oldest in the world still in use. The hill is not covered with olive trees, but presents a slightly bleak face with its rocky outcrops, some patches of green, and, of course, the sprawl of graves and headstones. Down at the foot of the Kidron Valley are two structures of interest. One has a conical roof and is called Absalom's Tomb. The other has a pyramid-

In this church is the Rock of Agony, where tradition asserts that Jesus sweated blood. This is a natural part of the rock on which the church stands.

Just above the Church of All Nations stands the Russian Church of St Mary Magdalene, with its cluster of golden, onion-shaped domes. It was built by Czar Alexander III in 1888 and, perhaps naturally enough, reflects the style of the churches built in Moscow in the 16th and 17th centuries. Some people regard this as the most superb church in Jerusalem and at night, when it is floodlit, with the domes and crosses gleaming through the dark trees, the church does have considerable glamour.

Before leaving to look at contemporary Jerusalem, one further

Top: sunset over the Negev Desert, (above) a young nature lover near Jerusalem and (remaining pictures) the varied terrain of the Judaean Mountains, which support sheep (facing page bottom) and arable farming (top right), almond trees (right) and an abundance of wild spring flowers (facing page top).

shaped roof and is cut in one piece directly from the rock of the mountain – this is known as Zachariah's Tomb.

In fact, neither has anything to do with the men from the Old Testament after whom they are named, but are believed to be the tombs of wealthy 2nd-century citizens of Jerusalem. However, time and observance have sanctified the monuments and they are certainly impressive.

The Garden of Gethsemane is a little further along the road which travels the base of the Mount of Olives. It is said that the olive trees one can see there now are old enough to have been there when Jesus was arrested. The Franciscan Church of All Nations is here, built in 1924, with many small domes, each dedicated to one particular country which helped to sponsor it. It is built on the site of a 4th-century Byzantine chapel.

site needs consideration. This is what is called the Garden Tomb, to which an interesting story is attached. In 1883, the British General Gordon (he of Khartoum), looking from the northern wall of the Old City (near the Damascus Gate), was impressed by the skull-like definition of the rock-face opposite. This insight created in him the conviction that this was where Christ was crucified (and not the traditional site in the Church of the Holy Sepulchre already

described). As a result, a garden on the rock was purchased and dedicated.

Only years later did excavations on the site reveal evidence that this was once indeed a garden which had contained all the circumstantial elements in the story of the death, burial and resurrection of Christ.

Today the Garden is a peaceful enclave in the bustle of east Jerusalem and is most pleasant to visit. Nobody tries to insist that this is the actual place of Jesus' death and burial, but interesting evidence is there.

A glance at a street map of Jerusalem will indicate that the modern city stretches out to the west and south of the Old City and that all the religious sites and memorials are concentrated in the Old City and immediately around its walls.

In fact, until 1860 nobody lived outside the city walls at all, though there were one or two monasteries. At this time the Jewish quarter

Facing page top: fruit and (left) antiques in a market in Jericho, site of historical treasures such as the ruined 8th-century Hisham's Palace (top and facing page bottom) and the Mount of Temptation, topped by a Greek Orthodox monastery (above), reputedly the setting for Christ's temptation by the Devil.

of the Old City was extremely overcrowded, and the English-Jewish philanthropist Sir Moses Montefiore promoted the first housing development outside the walls. After a wary start the logic of this was

accepted, and by the end of the century there were some ten Jewish settlements established.

Today, western Jerusalem is a busy, up-to-date, thriving city with modern thoroughfares, shopping centres, high-rise apartments, tower-blocks and offices. Among all this the old, original settlements still remain, sometimes in dilapidated condition, sometimes as artistic 'old world' pockets. In many ways, western Jerusalem is not unlike any other hot, Middle-Eastern city, with its dusty streets, busy markets, fast-food stalls and open-air cafés where one can just sit and gaze at the passing throng – but the mix of characters passing is probably greater than in most places, ranging from Arabs in their colourful, flowing robes to the severely-dressed, devout orthodox Jewish religious sects; from tourists to the young Sabras energetically pursuing a careerist course of upward mobility.

There is a friendly rivalry between Jerusalem and Tel Aviv, with

Above: the Nebi Mussa Mosque, south of Jericho, under which Muslim legend holds that Moses is buried. Facing page: (top) the monastery on the Mount of Temptation, and (bottom) the Monastery of St George, perched on a wall of the deep Wadi Qelt gorge, near Jericho.

the latter regarding itself as sophisticated and exciting and seeing Jerusalem as backward and solemn. There is a superficial truth in this contrast – for many reasons, Tel Aviv does give the impression of a hedonistic playground. But Jerusalem has its own style and the range of excellent restaurants from all nations, for example, is rapidly expanding.

What modern Jerusalem does have – apart from history and a thrilling atmosphere of ancient times – is some superb modern

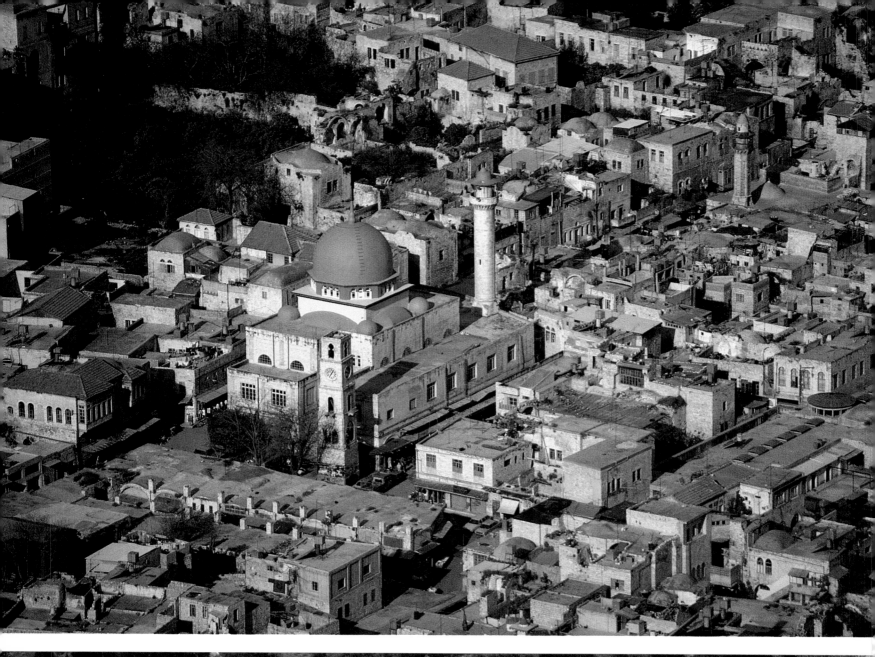

architecture. The Israel Museum, the Knesset (parliament) and the Hebrew University – all in the southwestern sector – are splendid examples of their kind. The museum, for example, which was opened in 1965, is divided into several sections. To house the Dead Sea Scrolls the magnificent Shrine of the Book was built, taking its shape from the pots in which the scrolls were discovered. The celebrated Japanese architect, Isamu Noguchi, designed the Billy Rose Sculpture Garden (the gift of the New York showman, who was a major collector). The range of the Museum's collection is enormously wide, moving from the most ancient of artefacts to modern paintings.

Outside the Knesset stands the large bronze Minorah – the seven-branched candelabra which is Israel's national symbol, and nearby burns an eternal flame in honour of fallen Israeli soldiers. An essential visit for all visitors to Jerusalem must be to Yad Vashem, the memorial to the six million Jews massacred by the Nazis in the Second World War. The museum traces events from Hitler's assumption of power in 1933 through the following 12 years.

Facing page: (top) the town of Nablus, around which lie such interesting sights as Jacob's Well, enclosed by a partly-built Greek Orthodox church (bottom), and the ruins of Samaria (top and above), which was the capital of Israel in 876 BC, was destroyed three times, and taken and renamed Sebastia by Herod in 27 BC. Left: fertile land near Jericho.

There are photographs and drawings from the concentration camps and works – including sculptures – made by people who died in the camps. There is a Hall of Remembrance and the whole establishment creates a darkly-powerful impression.

As we have seen, Jerusalem itself attracts members of the three main religions, and also representatives of innumerable denominations within them. Mostly they live easily together, though sometimes there are arguments over anything from the most trivial issue to much more important things. Among the Jewish denominations is one which is ultra-orthodox and, by demonstration

and lifestyle, marks itself off from the more progressive and secular communities.

This sect lives in an area called Mea She'arim and has an estimated 1,000 members, who live the lifestyle of a Polish shtetl (or Jewish village) in the 18th and 19th centuries. They dress accordingly, the men in black, broad-brimmed hats, sometimes in white stockings and black breeches caught below the knee. Women wear all-covering clothes and some married women shave their heads and use wigs or tightly knotted scarves around their heads. The atmosphere of Mea She'arim is intense and solemn, with pedestrians walking with a purposeful stride and men arguing seriously on religious matters.

It may seem strange to suggest that the tourist visits Mea She'arim to goggle at these devout people, but the neighbourhood

Olive and citrus groves adorn the hills of Samaria, among which nestles a grey stone village (top) and the ruined theatre of Sebastia (above left). Above: the Jordan River, (facing page) Nablus, lying between Mount Gerizim and Mount Ebal, and (overleaf) the tel of the town of Bet Shean.

is so unique and offers such an interesting insight into history that the thoughtful visitor will certainly value the experience.

One word of warning though. The community of Mea She'arim carries high and strict standards relating to dress, manner and observation of the Sabbath and demands it of others who walk their streets. A banner hung across the main thoroughfare, for example, reads: 'Jewish Daughter – The Torah obligates you to dress with modesty. We do not tolerate people passing through our streets

immodestly dressed.'

So visitors are warned. Decent, all-covering clothing is necessary; it is considered unsuitable to show affection in public, so people are not advised to walk arm-in-arm or even hand-in-hand.

Jerusalem will keep any visitor for several days, but it is well worth taking a day trip out of town. We have already looked at the more important sights which lie to the south, in the desert of Judaea, of which there are many. Journeying north does not overwhelm the traveller with ancient relics and towns so much, but does offer yet another facet of this land of contrasts.

Nablus is the town to make for and the journey here (it is just 29 miles (46 kms) from Jerusalem) takes one through Samaria, which has a quite different feel to it from Judaea. Samaria is greener, more pastoral; there are cypress and orange groves, vines, wild flowers and an overall impression of lushness. There is widespread farming and the pace is tranquil.

North of Jerusalem, the first town of interest is Ramallah. This is an elegant town which, because of its situation and fine climate, was always popular with wealthy Jordanians and Arabs as a winter resort,

Left: almond trees and (top) vines growing in the luxuriant Jordan Valley, where many varieties of flowers (above) are grown for export. Facing page: sunset glinting through an olive tree in the Judaean Desert.

and has wide streets and fine houses with large, attractive gardens. King Hussein of Jordan had a holiday home here.

There are many sites with biblical associations around here, such as the place where Jacob dreamed about his famous ladder, and Shiloh, recently excavated and an important Israelite shrine. There are also isolated ruins dating from the period of the Crusades.

Further north lies Nablus, the largest city in the area and now essentially an industrial and trade centre, with all that implies. One of its main industries is the manufacture of soap. But the surroundings and suburbs are very pleasant, with stone houses (re-tiled roofs, coloured shutters) and plenty of plants and other greenery.

Historically, Nablus is regarded as the site of the biblical

Shechem, where Abraham entered the Promised Land and made his first sacrifice to God. Near this site are Jacob's Well (inside a Greek Orthodox monastery) and Joseph's Tomb (set behind a large mulberry tree). And rising to dominate its surroundings is Mount Gerizim which was – and still is – the centre for the Samaritans.

The Samaritans are mentioned in one or two parables in the New Testament and, at the time of the Second Temple, they were the non-Jewish descendants of people from the north who wanted to help build the new temple but were rejected by the Jews. They moved to

Mount Gerizim and, seeing it in much the same way the Jews saw Mount Moriah, built their temple there. In Roman times there were many thousands of them, but persecution and war reduced their number. Today there are about 600 Samaritans proper, mostly living in this area, their schism with the Jews virtually forgotten.

On the summit of Mount Gerizim are several sites: a modern Samaritan synagogue, a slab of rock reputed to be where Abraham intended to sacrifice Isaac, and the ruins of a Byzantine church.

Today, the Samaritans still observe a Passover sacrifice on the summit of Mount Gerizim according to the style described in the Book of Exodus. This involves the ritual slaughter of a sheep in the presence of all the men of the community dressed in white.

Nearby is the village of Samaris (also called Sebastia or Sebaste), which is where the capital of the northern kingdom of Israel was established. There are some Israelite remains, and also artefacts from the Herodian and Crusader periods. In Roman times this was a thriving city, with an amphitheatre and columned streets

The summit of Mount Tabor (facing page top), which rises abruptly for 1650 feet above the Valley of Jezreel, is considered to be the place where Jesus was transfigured before Peter, James and John. Lying to the west of Mount Tabor is the Galilean town of Nazareth (remaining pictures) where Jesus spent most of his youth.

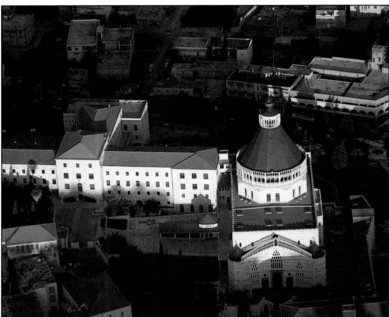

Above and top pictures: the Basilica of the Annunciation, built over the grotto where Gabriel delivered the annunciation to Mary, and (right) the entrance to the Old Synagogue where it is thought Christ prayed, in Nazareth. Facing page: (top left) Roman ruins at the ancient city of Ashqelon, (bottom left) the catacombs at Bet Shearim, and (top right) a statue interpreting the Holocaust, in Karmiel (bottom right).

of which remnants survive. Its main interest for Christian visitors is that it is believed to be the burial place of John the Baptist.

Kibbutzim and Moshauim

Modern Israel is, of course, world famous for the kibbutz movement. This is a system of communal settlements, the first of which – Degania at the southern end of the Sea of Galilee – was founded in 1909. Since then, they have grown in number and in prosperity although, despite their fame, kibbutzniks make up only four per cent of the total population.

Some kibbutzim are large, some small; some hold high ethical and religious standards, some are more secular in their approach; some are quite rich, some not so well off. But, irrespective of these differences, they all operate on the same basic principles. There is no coercion of any kind on the members who work together, share their property and eat together. Every member has a home on the kibbutz, and in some, children live apart in a children's house. This

aspect of kibbutz life has always been controversial, and today more and more children stay with their parents in the conventional style. But even so there is much less tying into family units than in the traditional methods of bringing up children.

Work on the kibbutz is shared equally, and every member takes his or her turn with the domestic chores – even those who may hold important posts 'outside' – many cabinet ministers have been kibbutzniks, for example.

All decisions, from the major to the minor – such as who does what work, who can travel where and who can study and so on – are discussed and settled by regular general meetings.

Every year, young people from all over the world come to spend some time working on a kibbutz in a voluntary capacity and to learn first hand about this exercise in practical communism. Their reaction depends a great deal on the atmosphere of the individual kibbutz, of course; sometimes they are given a comparatively easy time; sometimes they are given tough work and driven hard.

Quite a lot of kibbutzim run guesthouses – some quite excellent – and the traveller can stay at several. A lot are very well-equipped,

with swimming pools and very comfortable little houses.

Israel's other experiment in communal enterprise is the moshavim, which is a kind of combination of private enterprise and collectivism. In the moshav, each family lives in its own home, looks after its own land and handles its own financial affairs. However, the moshav collectively owns the agricultural machinery and buys in materials to the advantage of all the members.

This system proved most attractive to the waves of immigrants after the war, especially those who wanted to settle alongside people of their own language and culture and wanted to see the tangible results of their individual efforts. A second generation has now arisen which sees less problems with the mixing of basic national cultures. There are many more moshavim than kibbutzim in Israel today; in some cases, a moshav near a big city has become little more than a residential suburb.

The Jordan Rift: Jericho to Golan

The River Jordan rises in a series of icy springs from the slopes of Mount Hermon, on the Syrian border in the north of Israel. It gushes and rushes down the lower slopes, widening and slowing until it reaches the Sea of Galilee. At the southern end of the sea, the river follows the great rift valley, making its way at a leisurely pace between the hills of Jordan to the east and the hills of Samaria and Judaea to the west before easing its way into the Dead Sea. It runs through some of Israel's most beautiful landscapes, especially the fertile and pastoral areas of the north, and then meanders through more desert regions. Just south of the Sea of Galilee it becomes the actual border with Jordan. This makes access to one or two biblical sites difficult, but the visitor can find enough of interest along its banks to satisfy any needs.

The last great town it passes before reaching the Dead Sea is Jericho, which is famous for Joshua's destruction of its walls by the expedient of blowing trumpets. The city has been a magnet for archaeologists throughout this century. Much work has been done,

including the assembly of enough evidence to justify its title of 'the oldest city in the world'. However, so far nothing has been found which would suggest corroboration of the biblical saga.

In the Bible, Jericho is called 'the city of palms' and it still lives up to its name. It is a beautiful oasis of gardens, orchards, evergreens and hibiscus. Because of its warm but gentle climate, it was always a much-favoured resort, and even in winter, when nearby Jerusalem might be cold and wet, it remains mild enough for leisurely strolling or eating outdoors. The spring responsible for making Jericho a delicious oasis is called the Spring of Elisha or the Sultan's Spring. It is fed from an underground basin which collects winter rains from the hills of Judaea.

Opposite the spring (which has a pump-house) is Tel e-Sultan, which is the well-excavated site of old Jericho. Here is a curious round tower, made of stone, with a staircase, the purpose of which scholars have yet to decide. What they can tell us, however, is that it dates back to 8000 BC. On the western side of the town is the Mount of Temptation, flat-topped and with a wall around its summit. This is where, according to the New Testament, Christ, after he had fasted

Facing page: the hill of Megiddo, whose name has been corrupted to Armageddon from the Hebrew, Har Megiddo, where the New Testament states that the world's last battle will occur. Among the historical treasures found here are the ruins of a fort built by Solomon, a 4,000-year-old Canaanite temple, and a 9th-century water tunnel (above). Top: an ancient tomb in the catacombs at Bet Shearim (left).

for 40 days and 40 nights, was tempted by the Devil. The Greek Orthodox monastery perched on the cliff is 19th-century.

It is worth making a short detour to the north of Jericho to visit Hisham's Palace, the remains of which still manage to give some idea of the kind of lavishness that Jericho has always attracted. This palace was built in the 8th century for the caliphs of Damascus – they, too, enjoyed Jericho's mild winters. A surviving mosaic in the bath house illustrates the Tree of Life in brilliant colours.

East of Jericho is Allenby Bridge, one of the two crossing points over the river, and several monasteries built to house pilgrims who came to bathe in the river and take bottles of the water home with

them. It was here, reputedly, that Jesus was baptised, though another baptismal site has been suggested, near the Sea of Galilee.

Northwards from here, the Jordan Rift is largely barren. The river twists and turns on its way to the Dead Sea, and there is little of specific interest until one reaches the luxuriant fertility of the Valley of Bet Shean.

It is at this point that the Valley of the Jordan meets the Jezre'el Valley, which extends beyond the narrower Harod Valley off to the northeast and eventually the Mediterranean. The plain represents, therefore, the junction of two ancient routes and, as a result, Bet

Below: poppies growing near the Sea of Galilee (bottom), whose shores boast such sights as the Roman baths at Hamat Gader (left), famed for their mineral waters since ancient times, and Tabgha (bottom left), where Jesus multiplied seven loaves and a few fishes to feed 4,000 followers. Facing page: (top right) Mount Tabor, and (top left and bottom left) the ruined fortifications and (bottom right) the Old City wall in Tiberias, which was founded by Herod Antipas in AD 21 as the capital of Galilee.

After the fall of Jerusalem in AD 70 many Jews fled to Tiberias (facing page), on the western shores of the Sea of Galilee (above and overleaf), and established there an important seat of rabbinic learning which was eventually acknowledged as one of the four sacred Judaean cities.

Shean had a strategic importance, especially under the Romans. Today, it is an agreeable, if uneventful, town and pleasant enough to while away a few hours in.

The Bet Shean museum is worth a visit and so is the 6th-century Byzantine Monastery of Lady Marie, which has some beautiful mosaic floors. But perhaps the most impressive local structure is a Roman theatre constructed around AD 200. Although its upper storey has not survived, archaeologists have estimated that it must have held some 8,000 people. The vaulted entrance passages and stage are very well preserved.

The Sea of Galilee is 16 miles (25 km) north of Beat Shean, and around it the landscape changes dramatically, becoming green and richly fertile. It was not always so, but massive irrigation projects have brought abundance to the deserts: nowhere is this more in evidence than in this area and in the Jezre'el Valley (which we will explore later). There are date palms, citrus groves, banana and cotton plantations and the fruits and vegetables (celery, avocado, lettuce, courgettes) for which Israel is now famous.

Many kibbutzim have been established in the Galilee area, and they are frequently luxurious with trees, velvety-green lawns and gardens abundant with many flowers. On the way, pause by the Crusader castle of Belvoir, built in 1173. It has an impressive location and splendid fortifications, and is worth a visit if only for the spectacular views of the Jordan Valley it affords.

There could hardly be a greater contrast than that between the sun-bleached, parched deserts of the south of Israel and the fresh greenery of the area around, and to the north of, the Sea of Galilee. No matter how hot it may get in the summer months, the trees and flowers and, above all, the presence of water, make it an agreeable and comfortable place to visit.

As we have seen, many of the biblical sites in Israel are, inevitably, conjectural as far as their actual authenticity goes. Sometimes archaeological evidence has surfaced to support a long tradition; sometimes tradition is the only factor. But in the area of the Sea of Galilee, historical facts support the biblical stories.

The town of Capernaum, on the northern shore, was Christ's headquarters during his three-year ministry in Galilee. This is where he gathered his disciples, preached in the synagogue and performed the majority of his miracles. Migdal, the home of Mary Magdalene, is nearby, and so is the Mount of the Beatitudes (though the actual spot from which Jesus delivered the sermon is conjectural).

The Hebrew name for the Sea of Galilee is Kinneret, which was the name of an important town once located on the northern side.

Facing page: (top) fishing boats at En Gev and (bottom) the Church of St Peter's Primacy at Tabgha, where Jesus conferred the primacy of the Church upon Peter, both on the shores of the Sea of Galilee (centre left). Left: restoring a mosaic in Tabgha's Church of the Multiplication, and (above) zodiac signs on a mosaic floor at Hamat Tiberias (top left), the site of ruined, ancient synagogues and early settlements, in Tiberias (overleaf).

Later, it was called Lake Tiberias, again taking the name from an important town on its shore. It is 14 miles (22 km) long and, at its widest, seven and a half miles (12 km) across, so visitors conditioned to expect a body of water called a 'sea', may be surprised by its modest dimensions. Similarly, the River Jordan itself is far less broad and majestic than it is depicted in story, legend and song. Overall, there is an intimate quality about the area which matches well with both its history and its present-day atmosphere.

Even in Roman times the lake attracted people bent on pleasure and relaxation. The main town here is Tiberias, created by Herod Antipas in AD 18. He wanted a magnificent city to rival any in the empire and equipped it with a palace, a huge theatre and pleasure gardens. Over the centuries, Tiberias was taken over by the Crusaders and the Turks, and in the 19th century was devastated by an earthquake.

Today, tourism is the town's essential industry, with windsurfing and water-skiing available on the lake and luxurious modern hotels.

There is a glamorous waterfront with many open-air restaurants at the water's edge, where the speciality is St Peter's fish, fresh from the lake, which must be eaten off the bone to be properly appreciated. A leisurely meal here at dusk is a wonderfully civilised pleasure, with the Golan Heights opposite fading into darkness and the water lapping the strings of lights marking the coastline.

With such a long and varied history there are, inevitably, many ancient remains and monuments in Tiberias, with artefacts from the Roman, Byzantine and Turkish periods. However, most of the towers and walls which are such a feature of the town were built by the Crusaders.

Just over a mile (2 km) to the south of Tiberias is Hammat, which means 'hot springs'. Here are the hottest mineral springs in Israel, which have been known and used since Old Testament times and have made the town a celebrated health resort. Today, the spa complex is modern and well equipped. There is a top-class sanatorium and clinic, but warm pools (indoors and out) are available for holiday-makers, surrounded by pleasant lawns and with a restaurant.

Looking out over the northwestern shores of the Sea of Galilee, a beautiful Italian church (facing page) perches on the Mount of the Beatitudes, marking the spot from which Jesus gave the Sermon on the Mount. He lived and preached for some time nearby, at Capernaum, where excavation has revealed the remains (this page) of a white limestone synagogue dating from the 2nd or 3rd century.

North of Tiberias is Migdal and then Tabgha, which is believed to be the spot where Jesus performed the miracle of the loaves and fishes. This episode is recalled in the mosaic covering the floor of the nearby Byzantine church. Then we reach Capernaum, with its outstanding, red-domed church.

From Tiberias we proceed north, up the Hula Valley, towards Dan and Mount Hermon. This is a well-watered area with the many streams and springs gushing from the hillsides to feed the Jordan. At Hula is one of the world's most important nature reserves, created between 1958 and 1979. There are small lakes, water meadows and acres of lush vegetation. It is primarily a bird reserve, although water

buffalo have also been introduced to the area. Right up to the north, almost on the Syrian border, is another nature reserve – Tel Dan – which is, if anything, even more spectacular. Here the River Dan rises in dozens of streams which rush and meander through thickets of vegetation, creating pools and waterfalls, before merging into one stream to feed into the Jordan.

There are well-posted nature trails (long and short) and admirable facilities for picnics. This is a favourite day-out spot for families from the many kibbutzim in the area, as well as for nature-lovers and bird-watchers from all over the world.

Snow-capped Mount Hermon dominates the landscape. Nimrod's castle, a massive medieval fortress, is here and the lower slopes of the mountain are marvellous for ski-ing (the actual peak and upper slopes are in Syria). From here, the Golan Heights (which are geologically separate) stretch down towards the south. They have been the scene of much military activity over the years, and the more northern slopes tend to be bleak and inhospitable.

The southern section has attracted more settlements over the years, and many of the original kibbutz settlements, including the first of them all, Degania and Kinneret, are to be found here. Also worth a visit are the spectacular Roman Baths at Hammat Gader, which

Facing page: (top) a view of the reclaimed Huleh Valley, once a malaria-infested swampland and now a luxuriant nature reserve, and (bottom) the ruined Jewish stronghold of Gamla, both in the ruggedly-beautiful Golan Heights (below) of northeastern Israel.

were constructed in the 2nd century on a massive scale, full of opulence and decoration. Despite the ravages of earthquakes, much of the building survives, and the design and layout of the spa can be appreciated today. The warm waters can be enjoyed by the modern visitor and the area has been landscaped into a well-equipped leisure centre with pools, gardens, picnic facilities and even an alligator farm!

Among the scenic treasures of the Golan Heights is the Dan Nature Reserve, through which flows the Dan River (above), one of the three sources of the Jordan. Another source is the Banias Spring, which forms a silvery waterfall (facing page) near Kibbutz Snir.

The Jezre'el Valley and Nazareth

Nazareth is disappointing. As the childhood home of Christ and the

scene of the Annunciation it is – along with Bethlehem – one of the major points of reference for the spiritually-inclined visitor. The image is of a quiet, unspoiled little village nestling among the hills of Lower Galilee, full of sights and sounds that might evoke images of the New Testament stories.

Reality is different. There are sights and sounds in abundance,

Facing page: sunset near the ruins of Gamla in the Golan Heights, whose varied terrain includes snow-capped Mount Hermon (top) and the green Huleh Valley (above). Overleaf: an aerial view of Zefat, the capital of Upper Galilee and one of the four sacred Judaean cities.

but they are the inevitable sights and sounds of a modern, bustling town; a cacophony of traffic intermingled with the shouts of street traders. Nazareth is particularly busy on Saturdays, when the markets are in full swing.

Nor is it a particularly attractive town. Situated in a valley, its conglomeration of stone houses and buildings is surrounded by agreeably-green hills, sometimes sprinkled with flowers. But the architecture is not particularly interesting and the overall impression is of a prosperous town more concerned perhaps with tomorrow than

with yesterday.

However, it is a sacred site and it has a long and turbulent history. The modern Hebrew word for Christians is Notzrim, which comes from the town's name. An agricultural settlement for thousands of years, it was sacked by the Romans, by the Byzantines, the Persians and the Moslems, and later many of its churches were re-built by the Crusaders. Napoleon captured it in 1799 and it was the German HQ in the area at the outbreak of the First World War.

Called Ptolemais under the Egyptians, Acre (these pages) has changed its identity many times through its long history, having been a Roman colony, a Byzantine bishopric, an Arab fort and a Crusader capital. Its finest years were under the governor Jazzar Pasha, who virtually re-built the city, adding the Great Mosque (facing page).

Upper Nazareth is the new suburb in the hills above the town. Begun in 1957 it is now a flourishing industrial area with car, textile and furniture factories. Nazareth contains a number of places worth a visit, including the Frank Sinatra Club and Social Centre, funded by the singer, and the Basilica of the Annunciation.

This – the biggest church in the Middle East – is actually a modern building. It was designed by Giovanni Muzio of Milan and consecrated in 1969. Its conical grey dome dominates the town.

The cave dwelling where Mary is believed to have lived and, therefore, where the Angel Gabriel appeared to her, is in the lower part of the church, and this particular site has been identified and revered as such for nearly 2,000 years. A Byzantine church rose here in the 5th century; 600 years later the Crusaders re-built it, and a Franciscan church (built in 1730) was demolished in 1954 to make way for the modern building.

So the history is there, and the basilica reveals details of it. In the underground section of the church are Byzantine and Crusader remains (along with modern stained glass windows). The church is also a kind of repository of art from all countries of the world, gifts of Catholic communities. These make for fascinating study as each representation of the Annunciation theme takes on the national characteristics of the donor.

There are Oriental designs from Thailand, and the Canadian panel shows Mary set against the Rocky Mountains. There is a museum attached, which exhibits many of the artefacts found in local excavations. The nearby church of St Joseph is also built on top of underground caves, one of which has been designated the carpenter's workshop.

As in so many of Israel's other holy places, Nazareth contains many different denominations, and sometimes there is considerable rivalry between them. You will find, for example, a modern building called 'Mary's Well'. The actual well (Nazareth's natural source of fresh water) is within the Greek Orthodox church of St Gabriel. This, it is asserted, is the site of the Annunciation, the angel appearing to

Situated on a promontory on the northern end of Haifa Bay and washed by the blue waters of the Mediterranean, Acre has been much sought after for its fine harbour since biblical times, when it was an important Canaanite port. Today, it is sought by tourists lured by its graceful Old City and the delicious seafood served at its waterfront cafés.

Mary when she went to the well to draw water. The church is richly furnished and decorated, and the spring which feeds the well can be seen.

Since it is so busy and the pace is so hectic, a visit to Nazareth can be tiring, especially since all the streets seem to be constructed on hills. But the visitor can have a lot of fun browsing and haggling in the souk, or window-shopping along the main streets.

Nazareth is just off the Jezre'el Valley, which is the most highly cultivated part of Israel. It is clearly defined, but a narrow valley at the western end connects it with Haifa, Acre and the Mediterranean, while at the eastern end the Harod Valley links it with the Jordan Valley. It has always been, therefore, a significant part of an

important cross-country route.

Development of the valley was not undertaken until the early years of this century, when malarial swamps had to be cleared. Today it is a richly-agricultural area. The view from Mount Tabor, which is a few miles east of Nazareth, reveals a plain of patchwork fields, tree-lined roads, bushy hillsides and glimmerings of lakes and rivers. It is a triumph of irrigation and dedication.

The valley's main towns are Megiddo, Afula and Bet She'arim. Ancient history is very near the surface in this area and excavations continue. Every town and spring has its own memorials of the past to show: water systems, olive presses, synagogues and catacombs. None are more impressive, though, than those at Bet She'arim, where the catacombs are made up of a series of linked chambers – the largest has 24 rooms which contain more than 200 stone coffins, some of which weigh up to five tons. Apart from the strong connections with the life of Christ, this area is also interesting since it reveals so much about Jewish life in the 2nd and 3rd centuries.

Among other places of particular interest to the biblical traveller is Cana (Kafr Cana) which is where Jesus performed his first miracle, turning water into wine at a wedding feast that was running dry. Again we find Catholic and Greek Orthodox churches, each claiming to be built on the actual site of the miracle.

The focal point of Haifa, Israel's largest port, is Mount Carmel (bottom), the site of the distinctive, golden-domed Bahia Shrine (bottom left) and Elijah's Cave (below), where the prophet is thought to have hidden when fleeing from Ahab. Above the cave is the beautiful church of the Carmelite Monastery (facing page).

Beyond Bet She'arim the valley narrows and, with Mount Carmel on one side, takes us to Haifa and the sea.

On Holiday

It was a balmy Mediterranean evening. We had dined by the poolside

HA G ALIQVANDO SPELVNCAM INCOLVIT
MAGNVS ILLE PROPHETARVM DVX ET PATER
ELIAS THESBITES

Facing page: the magnificent Italian Renaissance-style ceiling in the church of the Carmelite Monastery and (above) the Bahia Shrine, which is the mausoleum of the Mirza Ali Muhammed, both in Haifa.

at one of Ashkelon's luxurious hotels and decided to walk along the beautiful beach under the stars. In the distance we could see a beach café, brightly lit, full of people obviously having a wonderful time.

A young man appeared and prevented us from entering. He was polite, charming, but determined we should not go in. We pressed for a reason why not, and eventually he drew one of us aside to explain that a family of Moroccan Jews was holding a circumcision party and

he thought that the young lady in our group might be upset.

When the young lady assured him that this was far from the case, he ushered us inside, gave us drinks and we were made very welcome at this intimate family ceremony. There was Arab music and Arab delicacies and we made several friends.

The holiday maker in Israel can stick to the well worn tourist itineraries, and absorb the sites and landscape. But there is every opportunity to get to know a little about its people too. After a brief, preliminary skirmish of politeness, barriers cease to exist; one can learn of family traditions, ceremonies and religious observance; discover the folk songs and dances of the country; try food very different from that usually offered in cafés and restaurants. Since

most Jewish Israelis are from one or other middle-eastern country, the cultural mix is fascinating.

Perhaps the chief focus for any visitor to Israel is to experience its

Left: Mediterranean waters buffet the crumbling Crusader fortress of Atlit near Haifa (remaining pictures). As well as being Israel's prime industrial centre, Haifa is a pleasant, leafy city of culture and sophistication, where inhabitants enjoy fine restaurants, smart shops and chic residences.

rich biblical associations – the country is so rich in associated memories that it is impossible not to. But too much study can be wearisome and some variety is called for. The active can find their sporting needs fully catered for, from skiing up on Mount Hermon to the magical underwater world of Eilat; there are nature trails among rivers and waterfalls for bird and animal lovers.

But sometimes one simply wants a day or two of pure, unadulterated leisure, away from the ancient stones and precious ruins. Israel can offer the perfect environment for this, too. Its Mediterranean coast, from Acre down to Ashkelon, is virtually one

Facing page top: the coast near Netanya, one of Israel's fine beach resorts, some of which offer more than sun, sea and sand. Ashqelon, for example, boasts a park containing Roman remains (this page), and at Caesarea (facing page bottom) a Roman aqueduct runs alongside the scalloped shore.

experience a bit of everything; absorbing the sights, travelling in ways which will enable him to meet the people, enjoying the smart nightlife of Jaffa and relaxing in the mesmeric silence of a boat on the Sea of Galilee, or bounding in the waves which crash down on those golden beaches.

long, golden beach and the string of towns – every one of them rich in history – shows a sophisticated, sometimes even slightly raffish, face very different from the towns of the country's interior.

So the holiday-maker has a rich choice. Ideally, he should try and

The Mediterranean Coast: Acre to Ashkelon

Ancient stone walls are reflected in the calm waters on which gaily-

painted boats lazily sway. Above a pile of rooftops, tiled and domed, the slender spikes of minarets reach for the blue sky. The houses themselves – pale, sandy-coloured – have blue and pink painted shutters. People wander lazily along the waterfront, perhaps pausing for a dark, thick coffee in a café beneath a cluster of striped umbrellas.

This could be a typical scene in any small fishing port around the whole of the Mediterranean. Only the minarets, perhaps, hint at an unusual flavour and give an Oriental feel to the quiet harbour.

For this is Acre, the most picturesque of all Israel's coastal towns.

has been carefully restored. This is a sequence of rooms, vaulted and supported by vast columns, which were used as an administrative centre and as living quarters. It is said that this is one of the oldest Gothic buildings in the world, but be that as it may, it is certainly one of the most impressive. At the lowest level is the crypt – actually a large hall used for ceremonial receptions and where, tradition asserts, Marco Polo was received on his voyage to China. One exit from the complex takes the visitor through a narrow, medieval secret tunnel out into the open air.

Acre is a gift to photographers, with its quaint clusters of buildings,

Facing page top: an aqueduct near the coast north of Acre, and (remaining pictures) Roman remains at Caesarea, which originated in the 3rd century BC as a small Phoenician port, and rose to fame in 22 BC when it became Palestine's capital under Herod the Great. He transformed the city with great feats of building and engineering, including fine palaces, a deep sea harbour and a magnificent amphitheatre (above).

and for centuries the most important. A glance at a map shows that Israel's Mediterranean shoreline is long and straight, undisturbed by bays, inlets or coves, except here, where the Bay of Acre provides a natural harbour. The bay is also beautiful, and the view of Acre, across its bay, is one of the more pleasant sights as one approaches from Haifa, passing through that town's hinterland of industrial estates (which is large and important but not very glamorous). In ancient times, Acre was the most important port of the eastern Mediterranean.

The town's original name was Akko (by which it is still known today), but was called St Jean d'Acre by the Crusaders who took it in 1104, and so it is known by this name in the west. Acre's Old City lies within a walled promontory on one end of its bay; on one side the waves crash against the old stones, on the other all is calm and peaceful.

The most immediately-notable building is the Mosque of Ahmed el-Jazzar, which was built in 1781 on top of the remains of the cathedral of the Holy Cross. It's beauty is renowned, with blue and brown murals and exquisite Persian carpets. In an upper gallery are preserved what are said to be hairs from the beard of the Prophet Mohammed.

But the real glory of Acre is the underground Crusader city which

quiet harbour, busy souk and evocative walks around the Old City walls.

The bazaars and arcades of small shops sell the usual mix of bric-a-brac and souvenirs, but watch out for the metalworkers, particular' those using copper. This is an industry typical of the area and the work it produces is mostly excellent.

South across the bay stands Haifa, one of the cities of which Israel is most proud. It is famous for having the only underground railway system in the country, and it is often described as the 'cleanest and greenest' of the country's cities. The greenness comes partly from its

Tel Aviv (these pages and overleaf) was founded in 1909 when a few Jewish families built homes on a stretch of land near the old port of Jaffa. Their settlement grew quickly into a bustling city, overtaking Jaffa, where the turrets and spires of old buildings, such as St Peter's Church (facing page top), still rise gracefully into the Mediterranean sky.

situation. It is built on the slopes of Mount Carmel and the natural vegetation of the mountain has been left within the developments. There are also pleasant parks and gardens.

Haifa is not mentioned in the Bible and, though it does have a long history, it was never a particularly important or distinguished settlement, despite its having a safe anchorage. It only really begins to arrive, as it were, in the 18th century, when the port began to develop and to set up competition with Acre. The city really took off

after 1918 with the development of major industries, the opening of railway lines and the building of the deep-water port which is so significant today.

The area around the port is the city's working place – industrial, busy and of little interest to the tourist. Higher up Mount Carmel, however, the atmosphere changes as one reaches the shopping centres, wide, tree-lined streets with cafés and entertainments and well-established residential areas. Even higher, almost at the summit, are the most sought-after residences – luxurious villas set in sparkling gardens. The universities are up here, too, and the Mount Carmel nature reserve. Here, there are forests, rocky paths, gorges and long, well-posted walks.

Although it has some 15 museums, many of which are devoted to science and industry, Haifa is less self-consciously historical than other cities in the country. In fact, its image is one of hard work and

achievement. There is an Israeli saying to the effect that Jerusalem studies, Tel Aviv plays and Haifa works!

King Herod the Great left his mark all over Israel in the form of ambitious and splendid architectural projects. Nowhere is this more apparent and impressive than at Caesarea on the coast to the south of Haifa. Until he took an interest, it was a small, unimportant port which had been built by Phoenicians in the 3rd century. Herod transformed it into a magnificent city complete with a deep-sea harbour, a splendid theatre, a temple, palaces and, as usual, an effective water system.

Miles of fine sand, sunny sea for water sports (above) and marinas (top and facing page top) for pleasure boats make Tel Aviv an ideal beach resort, and for history buffs there is the old town of Jaffa (facing page bottom and overleaf).

After a series of conquests and destructions by Arabs, Crusaders and many others, the town was eventually abandoned, the last time this happened being in 1948. Interest was revived again, however, mainly through the interest of Baron James de Rothschild, and Caesarea is now a well-heeled resort. There are luxurious villas,

One of Tel Aviv's most colourful sights is Carmel Market (these pages), where one's senses are assailed by the heady fragrance of fresh flowers and the tempting forms of succulent Middle Eastern produce, including the famous Jaffa oranges.

excellent restaurants, banana plantations, art galleries and the only golf course in Israel.

A great deal of restoration has been done to the Herodian remains, and the splendid monuments fit beautifully into the elegant atmosphere of Caesarea. The theatre is particularly impressive. Although seating fewer people than it did originally (since the upper galleries are missing), 2,500 can still enjoy the performances which are mounted there today – rock concerts and opera among them. A great deal of refurbishing has taken place, but even so considerable

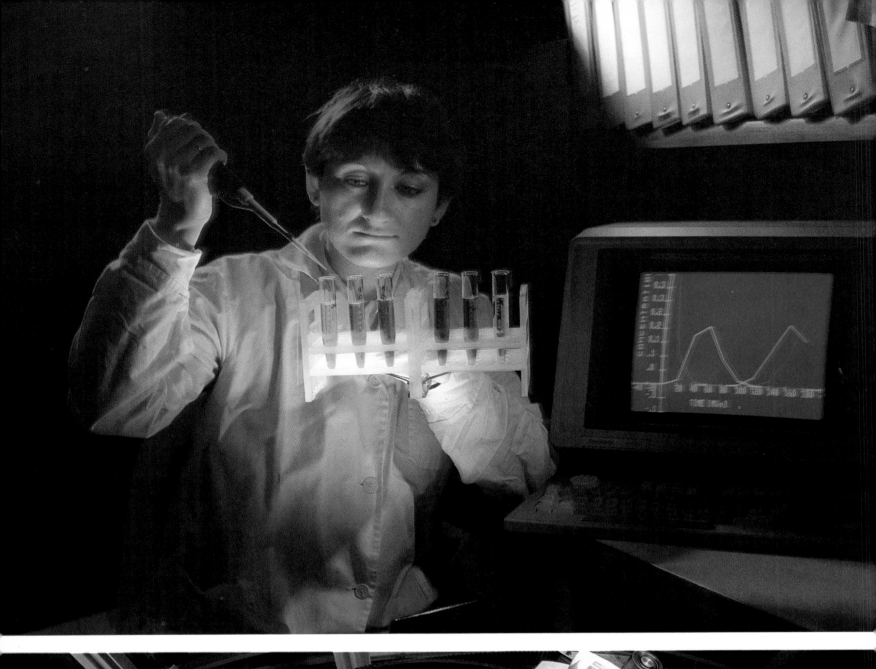

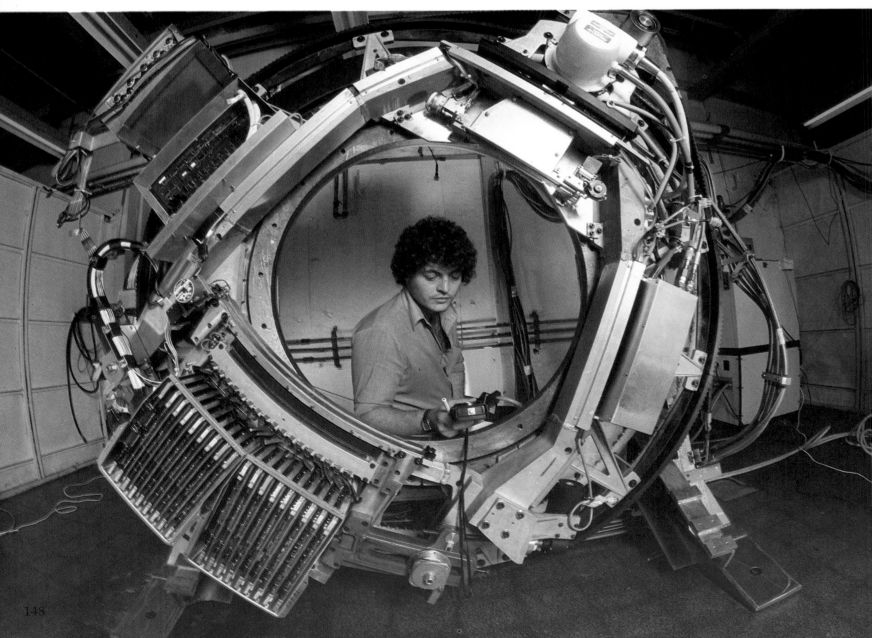

sections of the theatre are original. There are excellent views of the sea from most of the seats.

Another reminder of the Romans at play is the hippodrome, a stadium for chariot-racing and other athletic events. Herod's temple lies inside the Crusader city with its walls and moat. Here are some good examples of Crusader architecture, too, including the remains of a fine church.

But perhaps the one significant image every visitor takes away with him from this delightful spot is that of Herod's great aqueduct, which was built to bring water to Caesarea from Mount Carmel, eight

most popular resort, is here. It was founded in 1929 as a village for citrus farmers, and named after Nathan Straus who was the owner of the famous store, Macy's, in New York.

Continuing south along the coast one now reaches Israel's busiest and most extraordinary city – Tel Aviv. There is nowhere else remotely like it in the country. In many ways it seems to be yet another brash, crass concrete jungle stuck on the edge of a beautiful sea and enjoying wonderful weather. High rise blocks stand in ranks along the seafront, the urban sprawl extends further and further inland, the central areas are a constant jam of traffic and tourists among not very

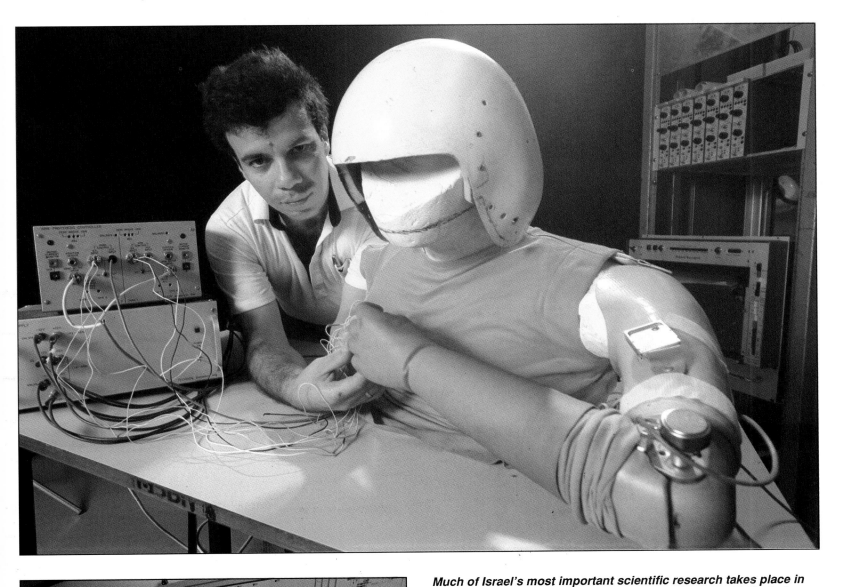

Much of Israel's most important scientific research takes place in Haifa, the home of Elcint, a hi-tech centre where sophisticated body scanners (facing page bottom) are developed, and the Technion Biomedical Faculty, where advances are being made in drug delivery systems (facing page top) and prosthetics (above). Left: a computerised grain silo in a kibbutz at Granot.

attractive buildings.

As we have already noted there is a definite rivalry between Jerusalem and Tel Aviv, the former regarding the latter as superficial and giddy, the latter regarding the former as stodgy and provincial. Yet Tel Aviv is smart and, to an extent, sophisticated; the shops are first-class and so are the restaurants. There is plenty of nightlife, not just cafés, discos and cinemas, but concerts, opera and drama, too. People who enjoy cities will recognise at once its gay self-confidence and sense of purpose.

Tel Aviv was deliberately created in 1909. Until then it was just another stretch of sand dunes on which the Mediterranean rolled its waves century after century.

Nearby is Jaffa, which is claimed to be the oldest port in the world, being founded by Japhet the son of Noah. It became important towards the end of the last century as early Jewish pioneers, pilgrims and travellers arrived. More and more arrived, many stayed and Jaffa grew. By 1909, many people were getting fed up with the overcrowded little town, so a group of Jews got together and bought a piece of land just to the north and began to build what is now Tel Aviv.

For various reasons, more Jews left Jaffa for the new town. There was an influx of immigrants from Poland in the 1920s, followed by German Jews fleeing the Nazis. This heavily-European presence explains much about the atmosphere of Tel Aviv and the

miles (13 km) away. A spectacular feat of engineering, a long section of this structure survives, striding across the coastal sand dunes.

Swimming is good here and there are chunks of Crusader and Roman masonry in the water. Coins and pottery can still be found in the sands.

To the south of Caesarea is the Sharon Plain, once famous for its forests and flowers. These have gone now, but Israel's imaginative development of modern farming techniques have brought it back to agricultural life. Behind the lines of sand dunes by the coast grow cotton, bananas, vegetables and flowers. Netanya, arguably Israel's establishment there of a pavement café society. Here, too, one finds more of the traditional European-Jewish food than anywhere else in Israel.

Today, many of the institutions created by the founders of the city have either been replaced or have disappeared. It was in Tel Aviv that David Ben Gurion read out the new Jewish State's Declaration of Independence in 1948 and, for a while, Tel Aviv was the capital. Jaffa and Tel Aviv became one city in 1950.

There isn't a lot to see in Tel Aviv. The visitor must take it as a place for simple pleasures. The beaches are grand and the swimming and surfing good; the nightlife is swinging and the restaurants excellent. But probably the greatest fun comes from the

as being too self-conscious and arty, but the renovations have been made with style and taste.

Jaffa also has a vivacious nightlife, with clubs offering everything from strippers and belly-dancers to traditional Israeli dancing, plus a selection of good restaurants which offer that interesting combination of fresh Mediterranean fish and Arabic salads.

South of Tel Aviv-Jaffa the white-gold sands stretch on down towards the Gaza Strip. An interesting detour is to Rishon Lezion, which is one of the centres of Israel's wine industry. It was founded towards the end of the last century by immigrants from Russia but was later patronised by Baron de Rothschild. In 1909, he handed his wineries over to the growers. There are guided tours of the cellars,

street-life – strolling, window-shopping, or sitting at a pavement café watching the passing parade. The main thoroughfare is Dizengoff Street (named after the city's founder and first mayor), and recently a new promenade has been built along the seafront.

Ancient Jaffa has been carefully restored and is now an attractive centre. With its towers, minarets and domes it has a distinctly Oriental appearance which is highly attractive. Part of the town is now an artists' colony, with studios, galleries and shops elegantly designed and displaying the best of modern art. It has been criticised

Jews, Arabs and, indeed, peoples from all over the world have settled in Israel and enriched the countenance of the country with a kaleidoscope of lovely faces (these pages).

and wine is available for tasting.

Israel makes excellent wine but it is not particularly well-known nor is it promoted at all vigorously in the country. The image of Israeli wine tends to be of the sickly, sweet stuff Jews tend to choose for

ceremonial occasions. But there is excellent Cabernet Sauvignon, Carignan, Semillon and Chenin Blanc. There are some sparkling wines and a local liqueur called Sabra which is gaining popularity in Europe.

Further down the coast is Ashdod, a seaport founded in 1957. It is heavily industrialised but has a beautiful beach. There are plans to develop its tourist potential in the near future, and it is projected as the third largest centre in Israel.

The last town of interest to the traveller on Israel's Mediterranean coast is Ashkelon, just on the edge of the Gaza Strip. It was one of the five main cities of the Philistine kingdom and has associations

Bottom: tomato harvest at Moshav Eidan, in the wilds of Arava. Moshavim are collective farming settlements similar to kibbutzim (these pages), which have proved to be the most successful form of communal living to date. Kibbutzim not only support themselves, but feed the country, grow produce for export and improve inhospitable land. Overleaf: an aerial view of a kibbutz in the Jezreel Valley.

with Samson and Delilah. Today, it is a resort town with elegant villas among the tamarisk trees, a wonderful beach and a couple of good hotels. In its national park are Roman statues, remnants of Crusader fortifications and the ramp of the 3,500-year-old city wall, all in position among the trees and greenery. The actual town (called Migdal-Ashkelon) is set a few miles inland and is a pleasant spot with an interesting market and mosque. It would be hard to find a better spot in which to relax from the hard-walking itineraries of dedicated tourism.

Our last memories of Israel were those of a glorious holiday —

Today, despite the development of mechanised farming in Israel, many smallholdings are still worked by hand. Facing page: (top) harvesting tomatoes on the West Bank, (bottom) an Arab woman leaving a field in the Jordan Valley, (top) ploughing in the traditional way, (above) picking dates and (top right) olives, and (right) a farm worker in the Wadi Qelt.

swimming in the Mediterranean, sunning on the silver beaches of Ashkelon, enjoying the glittery bustle of Tel Aviv's nightlife, sitting in an elegant fish restaurant watching the highly cosmopolitan world drift by in the sultry dusk.

But as the plane rises from Ben Gurion airport, taking us back to a chillier Europe, other memories crowd in, tiny vignettes drawn from this culture which is such a fascinating mix of the familiar and the alien, the Eastern and the Western.

There was that picnic of cheese sandwiches and a flask of coffee among the leaping, sparkling streams of the Tel Dan nature reserve, and then dinner at an Arab restaurant in Jerusalem where we sat on thickly carpeted floors and gazed transfixed as some 26 different dishes were set before us. There was drinking the juice of freshly squeezed grapefruit during the midday heat and, later, sipping the local white wine in the tree-shaded courtyard of our hotel.

Then there were the sights – not just the ancient buildings and holy places, but the spectacle of the varying scenery. One can watch the desert fade into night, a slowly melting spectrum of rose, ochre, cinnamon and misty blues; there are the lushly planted, almost tropical cultivated valleys growing spectacular flowers, cotton and bananas. There are massive walls, towers, viaducts and temples that have seen more history than any of us can imagine – and new factories, houses and docks pointing to the future.

And the people ... tiny children rushing up to have their photographs taken, for example. They didn't want pictures of themselves, they just wanted to be recorded by us, visitors from countries they only hear about. The sheer friendliness of the stall-holders in the bazaars (who relish a haggle over anything from a carpet to a straw hat), the young soldiers – male and female – whose

Facing page: fish ponds on the flat plains of the Jezreel Valley, which, due to its natural springs, was cultivated by many peoples throughout biblical times and has been the scene of countless battles for control of Israel. Above: harvesting and ploughing by the Sea of Galilee (overleaf).

sunny smiles and sheer pride in their country belie the uniforms and armoury. The severe looks and formal mien of the orthodox Jews, the exuberant mid-European enthusiasm of more recent immigrants.

For three of the world's great religions, Israel is The Holy Land and – despite the tourists, the guides, the souvenir sellers – it is easy to relax and get in touch with the brooding spirituality which hovers, ever-present. On the summit of Masada, outside the great Dome of the Rock, bustling along the Via Dolorosa or just sitting quietly in one of the many churches (and curiously, the actual denomination of the church seems irrelevant), memories of wars, factions, invasions and the violence of Israel's long history recede and for an hour or so it is possible to perceive a kind of essential tranquility that no other country can offer.